PRAISE

MANAGING LE

ANXIETY

"Anxiety may be one of the main reasons many pastors leave the ministry. . . . Steve offers a helpful, gospel approach to managing leadership anxiety. This is a book we all need to read."

RON EDMONDSON, CEO, Leadership
Network

"Steve Cuss leads you on a journey of discovery and practical approach that will literally change your relationship with worry and anxiety. Every parent and leader needs this book."

SHERRY SURRATT, executive director of
parent strategies, Orange

"Leadership isn't just what you do; it's who you are. Steve Cuss helps us develop that part of who we are that handles (or mishandles) anxiety. This book equips you for those moments when you realize things are beyond your direct control."

MARSHALL SHELLEY, director, Doctor of
Ministry program, Denver Seminary

"How we manage anxiety matters, and Steve provides wisdom for every one of us navigating the invisible forces impacting our work and our health."

REV. CHUCK DEGROAT, PhD, professor
of Pastoral Care and Christian Spirituality,
Western Theological Seminary

"Anxiety draws us into a downward spiral. We need outside help to break in and redirect our vision. Steve Cuss offers us that kind of fresh, honest voice to snap us out of the downward spiral. Not only will we become less anxious, we'll become more whole, hopeful, and fruitful. A much-needed resource for the church in these anxious times."

MANDY SMITH, author, *The Vulnerable Pastor*; pastor, University Christian Church

"Through guided personal reflection and system analysis, Steve imparts wisdom that will help leaders last and churches thrive. This will be a book our team works through!"

GLENN PACKIAM, lead pastor, New Life Downtown, NewLifeChurch.org

"This is a brilliant book. One to slowly digest and share with your team."

JUD WILHITE, senior pastor, Central Church; author, *Uncaged*; and
LORI WILHITE, founder, Leading and Loving It; author, *My Name Is Victorious*

"Steve has brought to the surface things that I have never read in any other leadership books."

DON WILSON, senior pastor, Christ's Church of the Valley, Accelerate Group

"Steve compares anxiety with tangled fishing line, an impossible mess. Impossible, that is, until you learn a few basic techniques to unpick things, one little bit at a time. This is a book to kickstart that process. This is a book that is the equivalent of the expert untangler, speaking softly and confidently in your ear, 'not that one; this one.'"

DR. CONRAD GEMPF, lecturer in New Testament at London School of Theology; author, *Jesus Asked* and *How to Like Paul Again*

"I have seen the power of genograms and differentiation in my own life. Steve takes these and many other tools to help us enter the world of noticing and moving through internal anxiety and group dynamics. This book is a great primer for anyone trying to grow in their understanding of how to lead in the anxious world we live in."

JAY PATHAK, pastor, Mile High Vineyard;
coauthor, *The Art of Neighboring*

"I have struggled with anxiety all my life, and the only way I have learned to live with it is not to fight it away, but to invite God to be with me in it. That is exactly what Steve Cuss helps you to do in this book. This book will be a great guide as you walk with others and with your own mind on the hard road worn by anxiety into deeper and deeper freedom."

LAURA TURNER, journalist

"If you want to grow as a leader, then *Managing Leadership Anxiety* is a must-read. The principles laid out in this book are responsible for the transformation of many of the leaders in my own community. Steve is the real deal as he is a practitioner as well as a thought leader."

DAVE RUNYON, coauthor, *The Art of Neighboring*

"Steve Cuss clearly identifies the reality of emotional undercurrents in ourselves and others that stonewall connection and real progress. Steve is a needed voice among leaders today. If you want to build a culture of trust, connection, and impact in your home or organization, then you need to read this book."

DAVE DUMMITT, lead pastor, 2|42
Community Church; cofounder, GYVE

"Every Christian will benefit from reading this book. Pastors, seminarians, and congregational leaders will find this an especially helpful resource."

JIM HERRINGTON, author and founder,
The Leader's Journey

"If you have been entrusted with the responsibility of leading any group of people, you owe it to yourself and to them to read this insightful book."

LUKE NORSWORTHY, pastor, author, and podcaster

"In *Managing Leadership Anxiety* Steve helps us look under the hood and not only trouble shoot but repair the often overlooked sources of anxiety in us as leaders, the teams we lead, and the organizations we serve."

GENE APPEL, senior pastor, Eastside Christian Church, Anaheim, California

"Steve Cuss is an authentic pastor and a tremendous leader. He's been one of my 'go-to's' when I have anxious seasons. The principles he shares will become tools that you return to again and again."

CALEB KALTENBACH, founder, The Messy Grace Group; author, *Messy Grace*

MANAGING LEADERSHIP ANXIETY

LEADERSHIP NETWORK

MANAGING
LEADERSHIP
ANXIETY

Yours and Theirs

STEVE CUSS

THOMAS NELSON
Since 1798

Published in Nashville, Tennessee, by Thomas Nelson. Thomas Nelson is a registered trademark of HarperCollins Christian Publishing, Inc.

Thomas Nelson titles may be purchased in bulk for educational, business, fund-raising, or sales promotional use. For information, please e-mail SpecialMarkets@ThomasNelson.com.

Any Internet addresses, phone numbers, or company or product information printed in this book are offered as a resource and are not intended in any way to be or to imply an endorsement by Thomas Nelson, nor does Thomas Nelson vouch for the existence, content, or services of these sites, phone numbers, companies, or products beyond the life of this book.

Unless otherwise noted, Scripture quotations are taken from the Holy Bible, New International Version®, NIV®. Copyright © 1973, 1978, 1984, 2011 by Biblica, Inc.™ Used by permission of Zondervan. All rights reserved worldwide. www.zondervan.com. The "NIV" and "New International Version" are trademarks registered in the United States Patent and Trademark Office by Biblica, Inc.™

Scripture quotations marked KJV are from the King James Version. Public domain.

ISBN 978-1-4002-1089-3 (eBook)
ISBN 978-1-4002-1088-6 (TP)

Library of Congress Cataloging-in-Publication Data

Names: Cuss, Steve, 1971- author.
Title: Managing leadership anxiety : yours and theirs / Steve Cuss.
Description: Nashville : Thomas Nelson, [2019] | Includes bibliographical references. |
Identifiers: LCCN 2018031236 (print) | LCCN 2018051465 (ebook) | ISBN 9781400210893 (e-book) | ISBN 9781400210886 | ISBN 9781400210893 (eBook)
Subjects: LCSH: Leadership--Religious aspects--Christianity. | Leadership. | Anxiety--Religious aspects--Christianity.
Classification: LCC BV4597.53.L43 (ebook) | LCC BV4597.53.L43 C87 2019 (print) | DDC 253/.2--dc23
LC record available at https://lccn.loc.gov/2018031236

Printed in the United States of America

23 24 25 26 27 LBC 28 27 26 25 24

About Leadership Network

Leadership Network fosters innovation movements that activate the church to greater impact. We help shape the conversations and practices of pacesetter churches in North America and around the world. The Leadership Network mind-set identifies church leaders with forward-thinking ideas—and helps them to catalyze those ideas resulting in movements that shape the church.

Together with HarperCollins Christian Publishing, the biggest name in Christian books, the NEXT imprint of Leadership Network moves ideas to implementation for leaders to take their ideas to form, substance, and reality. Placed in the hands of other church leaders, that reality begins spreading from one leader to the next . . . and to the next . . . and to the next, where that idea begins to flourish into a full-grown movement that creates a real, tangible impact in the world around it.

NEXT: A Leadership Network Resource
committed to helping you grow your next idea.

NEXT
LEADERSHIP NETWORK

leadnet.org/NEXT

CONTENTS

INTRODUCTION

All people *should strive to learn before they die,*
what they are running from, and to, and why.

—JAMES THURBER[1]

L eaders face a steady onslaught of internal and external pressures we are not trained to handle. We focus on skill development and hone our gifts but too often neglect the most powerful leadership tool: awareness of what is happening under the surface. All manner of triggers, reactivity, and stories we tell ourselves bubble just under our conscious awareness. This boiling collective blocks our capacity to be present because it takes energy to manage, especially when we're not aware of it or when we're reacting unconsciously to anxiety in someone else. When I first started leading twenty-five years ago, I was all gusto but unaware of what was happening underneath. I had mixed motives, a huge shadow, false assumptions, drives I couldn't name, and plenty of well-meaning blunder. I was also highly reactive to anxiety in others. I have stories . . . so do the people I was serving.

This book will help diagnose what is causing your anxiety and also provide you with prescriptive tools to help diffuse anxiety—moving you from being managed by anxiety to managing anxiety, both yours and theirs. You will become more self-aware, but becoming aware is only step one in the growth process. We all know people who are self-aware but do tremendous damage, or even people who use self-awareness as permission to stay the same. Awareness is critical to be sure, but it is not the path of growth, it is simply the gate. We unlock it and walk through it, but on the other side of self-awareness is difficult work that brings deeper freedom for us and those we serve.

This is no small journey.

A leader who discovers the cause of anxiety and uses the approach in this book to manage it has an increased capacity for anxious situations, difficult people, and ambiguity. By managing this bubbling cauldron, you can break through recurring patterns and lead in a more effective gear.

A leader is not the only person whose anxiety gets in the way. A group of people like a family or a staff can develop a systemic anxiety that keeps them stuck. Once we've covered some individual tools that help diffuse anxiety, we'll focus on group dynamics and how a leader can bring significant health to his or her team by addressing recurring relational patterns. You can notice not just your own or another's anxiety, but also your entire organization's or family's anxiety. Who always bulldozes over people, who gets the last word? Who stays silent and then calls a "meeting after the meeting" to talk behind others' backs? Most powerfully: How is your organization or family stuck in a chronic pattern? As you work through this material you will develop the capacity to notice not only your own anxiety, but also your entire group's anxiety.

If you become not only self-aware but also group-aware and lead beyond awareness, you can create a healthy culture for people to thrive.

This is where change and health really occur. If you become not only self-aware but also group-aware and lead beyond awareness, you can create a healthy culture for people to thrive. Whether you lead an organization, a family, or a department, or if you just want to understand a difficult relationship in your life, these tools can give you fresh ways forward. Many people have implemented these practices regardless of their position in a group and have seen healthy change.

Anxiety is contagious, which is why it shows up in groups as well as individuals. Have you ever had one of these situations?

- When someone is anxious, she talks to you about it, and now you are anxious about what she is anxious about.
- When you are leading a group and the group is highly anxious, people's anxiety may be feeding off the anxiety of one member or focusing on you because of change you are bringing.
- When someone massively overreacts to your leadership, either positively or negatively, he needs you to be someone that you are not. He is also projecting onto you expectations you cannot fulfill or blame that is not yours to own.
- When someone is anxious or hostile about another person, sometimes he is asking you to subtly or not so subtly join his team against the other.
- You struggle with personal anxiety unrelated to your leadership, and it affects the way you show up.
- Ongoing relational tension that either escalates with every encounter or is an ever-present reality just under the surface. Everyone knows about it; no one talks about it.
- When you don't know what to do when you have to make a decision because you are the leader, and you want more information or context, but it's time to make the call.
- You experience anxiety from making a well-meaning mistake that damages people. You tried your best but were wrong. You still need to lead, but you are licking your wounds. Critics are giving you feedback on the decision from the sidelines, yet what

stings most is they are technically right. They were uninvolved and nowhere to be found when you had to make the call, but they are technically right.

In all likelihood, a leader's bookshelf contains resources that attempt to address these types of situations but focus more on essential skills. Few of them get to the heart of why we show up the way we do, why certain people frustrate us, why we fall into predictable patterns, and why groups operate the way they do. Until we harness that power our leadership is stunted and never integrates from our whole person.

The concepts in this book do not require formal training or a particular personality—they simply require some courage to look under the surface and the desire to break free from chronic patterns and triggers. If you are on a quest for health and freedom or want to make sense of difficult relationships, you can benefit from the diagnostic and prescriptive tools in this book. It has a leadership focus because almost all of us interact with and influence others, so this book is for anyone from pastors to parents to marketplace leaders. This material moves us from places we are stuck toward deeper impact and cultural health. Many people write about burnout. This material presumes that burnout and leadership fatigue have more to do with anxiety and relational stuckness than workload.

Some final thoughts:

- I was not raised inside the church or any religious system, but I began following the teachings of Jesus of Nazareth when I was a teenager. If you are not a follower of Christ, you can benefit from this book. But my worldview is centered on the teachings of the New Testament, particularly Jesus of Nazareth and Paul of Tarsus. As I have studied family systems theory, also known as Bowen theory, I have discovered parallels between this provocative theory and the freedom that the "good news" offers.

- Anyone can read this book alone, but it is best engaged in dialogue and story sharing, so I recommend discussing it with a group. Some of the application tools in the later chapters require a group to help you process. I teach these materials at our church over nine months because a slow orientation around these concepts is essential to helping them stick. Most leaders like to move through a book quickly, so I offer exercises that range from a few minutes to a couple of hours. The busy leader who chooses to skim can still benefit from the material, but you will gain more if you engage with people you trust over a period of time.

- A thought about pronouns: In order to reflect my respect and appreciation for leaders of all stripes, I interchange *he* and *she* as I describe a leader. This feels a little clunky, but I much prefer the clunk over single gender pronouns. Hopefully the grammatical clunk won't trip you up as you recognize female and male leaders of all persuasions.

- I was born and raised in Australia, and although I have lived much of my life in the United States, I still operate from an Australian point of view and vocabulary. I have been able to make the change to US spelling and some pronunciation, but I cannot refer to someone's mother as "mom," so you will see a reference to "mum" once in a while. What can I say? Mum will always be mum, and I trust my North American readers will be able to translate.

- All the stories in this book are true, but I have changed names and some identifying details to maintain anonymity.

Ready? Let's go.

one

THE ANXIETY GAP

Between stimulus and response there is a space. In the space there is the power to choose our response. In our response lies our growth and our freedom.

—VIKTOR FRANKL

W hat do you do when you don't know what to do?

    This leadership journey began when I was twenty-four years old and had been married six days. It was my first day as a hospital chaplain at the University of Tennessee Medical Center in Knoxville. It housed six hundred beds, home hospice, and the only level-one trauma ER in the region, complete with a LIFESTAR medical helicopter. This was when people used pagers, and I was given three pagers to begin my twenty-eight-hour shift. One pager was for my units, one was for the emergency room, and one for the code team. That beeper buzzed violently and flashed bright blue anytime someone's heart stopped anywhere in the hospital. As one medical resident later put it, "The code team . . . when the patient's heart stops, yours starts racing."

So, first day on the job: slacks, dress shirt, comfy dress shoes, and a racing heart. The comfy shoes turned out to be the most important item, because hospitals are a giant maze of stairs and wards covering several surface miles, and a chaplain can clock three or four miles on any given day. My wife dropped me and my overnight bag off at the front entrance with a kiss, a prayer, and "I'll see you at lunch tomorrow; you're going to do great." The doors opened, and I walked into a foreign world. I had never seen a dead body before. I had very little experience with grief. I had just finished a bachelor of arts in Bible and preaching, and this was my first full-time ministry assignment.

I was participating somewhat by accident in clinical pastoral education, or CPE. It was by accident because my wife had one more year of college left, and I needed a job to provide for us. After looking into a few options, the local employment agency suggested I try chaplaincy. UT Medical Center just happened to be hiring its annual slate of chaplain residents, and in spite of my age, lack of experience, and lack of a graduate degree, they offered me the job. I didn't know what I was getting into, but the pay was enough to provide for us, and the experience sounded promising. I had no idea what an understatement that would become.

A chaplain resident is like a medical resident—you spend one year serving the spiritual needs of the hospital in a clinical learning environment. On that first morning the six new chaplain residents negotiated who got which departments of the hospital, and these departments became our "parish" for six months. For the second half of the year, we'd switch to another parish. We were the frontline response for any situation needing a chaplain. The permanent chaplain staff had other duties and would back us up as needed.

I was assigned the following: Pediatrics; Labor and Delivery; Neonatal Intensive Care; Pediatric Intensive Care; and the heart floor, kidney floor, and their respective intensive care wards. In the second six months, I served in Home Hospice and Home Health, Chemotherapy, Radiation, Pre- and Post-Surgery, Surgical Intensive Care, and on the medical ethics board. Most days the residents worked 8:00 a.m. to 5:00 p.m., but four to six times each month we worked a marathon shift from eight in the morning until noon the next day. The overnight chaplain covered the ER and code team for those twenty-eight hours and the entire hospital through the evening and overnight.

After assigning our wards, Randy, one of the supervisors, toured us around the hospital. We started at the top floor and slowly wound our way down, visiting every ward and meeting staff and patients. The tour was utterly overwhelming—odd smells lingered; medical tubes were everywhere holding weird-colored fluids; people walked around in all kinds of medical shape, mostly bad shape. The intensive care units were worse, and I couldn't keep eye contact with some of the patients. Then there was the pediatric intensive care unit with bald-headed kids fighting cancer and the neonatal intensive care unit with the smallest babies I'd ever seen. Within the first hour I was completely overwhelmed and wondered what sort of terrible mistake I had made when I agreed to this job.

Only the day before, Lisa and I had lazily left our honeymoon cabin in the Smoky Mountains and stopped by the grocery store to buy the first of everything a married couple needs: spices, toilet paper, and Tupperware. We needed three carts for all our stuff, and the receipt was two feet long. We proudly drove to our new home— married student housing—a 1970s single-wide trailer right on the French Broad River on the outskirts of Knoxville. Setting up our new home felt like we were real adults, but touring the hospital sobered me up to just how young and inexperienced I was.

As Randy finished our tour my blue pager started buzzing.

"Which one is the blue one again?" I asked.

"That's the code team. You need to go."

Right. The pager that says someone's heart has stopped. My heart had been racing for some time already.

And here, verbatim, is the full extent of the preparation I was given as a chaplain. I asked Randy, "What do I do now?"

"It will be interesting to find out, won't it?" he replied.

I looked at Randy, thinking he was teasing me, but he was serious. Kind, but serious. I waited a few more seconds in case he'd give me more instruction, but he was silent.

"But what if I make a mistake?"

"You are going to make hundreds of mistakes this year."

And with that little pep talk, I was on my own. I walked toward the intensive care waiting lounge but didn't need to check in to see where I was needed; I could hear the commotion as I approached. Someone had died, people were screaming, and I was supposed to do something about it.

What do you do when you don't know what to do?

Leaders are faced with countless situations where they only have a notion of what to do or partial information yet are required to act anyway. Most of the time leaders have to do something regardless of how equipped or ready they feel. I've read dozens of leadership books, and many of them define leadership. John Maxwell says that "Leadership is influence."[1] Marcus Buckingham says that "Leadership is rallying others to a better future."[2] Darcy Eikenberg defines leadership as "The courage to do the right things even when they are hard."[3]

These are all accurate and helpful definitions. I'll add mine: leadership is knowing what to do.

One of the simplest ways to know you are the leader in a group is that people look at you when they don't know what to do. When I toured the hospital and my beeper went off, I didn't know what to do, so I looked to Randy because he was the leader.

A few minutes later, I was in the intensive care waiting lounge, and everybody was looking at me because they did not know what to do. I was the presumed leader because I was the chaplain. Never mind that I didn't know what to do either; I needed to do something.

Leadership is almost always intuitive because leadership situations are fluid and dynamic. Most of the time we don't exactly know what to do. We end up with a gap between not knowing what to do and needing to do something.

The gap is one of the most uncomfortable places to live because a leader feels immense internal and external pressure to *do something*. In that gap all kinds of interesting things emerge: a bubbling cauldron of anxiety, fear, childhood trauma, the stories we tell ourselves, idols, and more. All of these show up in leadership environments. So as a leader lives in the gap, she is faced with three options: (1) run from it and give up leading because it is too uncomfortable; (2) fake it and pretend she knows what she is doing and thus build a chasm of hypocrisy; or (3) develop a capacity to "mind the gap."

Minding the gap, as you might imagine, takes some sweat and tears, but the result can be a deeper level of freedom. When you find yourself in this gap, take a pause rather than blazing forward. If you pause and tune in to your inner dialogue, anxiety, triggers, what makes you mad, *who* makes you mad, assumptions you bring into every leadership situation, how you manage mistakes and how they inform your leadership, you can be free of the recurring patterns that keep you stuck.

But not only that.

Equally interesting is the *emotional context* of every leadership situation. Because leadership involves at least one other person, it involves at least one other boiling collective. So, leadership becomes about the emotional context: yours and theirs. Managing anxiety under the surface: yours and theirs.

We begin by becoming more self-aware about how this unconscious material informs leadership. If a leader can think about the way he thinks, he can become a very powerful presence, able to understand himself and, most powerfully, able to become fully present to the people he is called to lead and serve.

Every leader will find herself in an unfamiliar situation, no matter how much formal training or experience she has. She will make mistakes, deal with conflict, and change her leadership style to adapt to the organization. Every leader can benefit from a set of tools that help develop a hyperawareness to what is going on under the surface, in the mind and in the body. This hyperawareness offers the leader a rare gift of being able to manage, rather than be managed by, all this subtext.

Have you ever gone into a meeting dreading the conversation you needed to have, so you played it out in your mind obsessively as if manic worry would help the meeting? Have you ever led a meeting and stepped on a land mine you didn't even know existed, and suddenly your well-intentioned leadership turned into hurt feelings and misunderstanding? Have you struggled to focus on the person in front of you because your mind was elsewhere? Have you brought a previous situation into the present? Have you felt shame over a mistake and wished you could have a do-over?

Any honest leader will answer yes to all these situations. They are the frequent experience for every leader, and I believe they are the cause for leader burnout. Burnout has less to do with workload and more to do with internal and external leadership anxiety. As surely as the sun rises every morning, so will a leader face a situation where she is anxious or annoyed at the person she is leading, or she wonders why she feels ashamed. Or he gets tired of being *stuck in the same pattern* with his team. Or he doesn't know what to do, yet he must do something.

That was the situation I faced after the code team pager went off.

I walked into a war zone of grief and death called the intensive care waiting lounge.

The intensive care waiting lounge is a large room full of recliners. Families set up camp in that room while patients fight for life on the other side of the wall. Because of the open nature of the room, the hospital built a very small corner room to offer privacy for doctors to meet with families when they need a medical update. Except it isn't like that at all. The small room isn't even a whole room—just four self-standing walls with no closed ceiling, lots of windows, and no privacy. I'm sure in the early days of the room's existence doctors pulled every family in for medical updates, but over time busy doctors decided to skip the effort if they had good news. Instead they'd just walk right over to the recliners and give the update in front of other families. If it was bad news, however, they'd walk over to the recliners and ask the family to come into the private room. This practice of selective updates in the small room caused families to name it the Death Room.

Burnout has less to do with workload and more to do with internal and external leadership anxiety.

I didn't know any of this at the time. I didn't know that the small room is the most hated and resisted room in the entire hospital. All I knew was that as I walked out of the elevator, there was screaming and wailing coming out of the small room. I felt everyone in the recliners looking at me as I walked in. The anxiety in me and around me was palpable. I could barely breathe.

I walked inside the room. There were more than a dozen family members, most of them screaming, and four or five doctors and nurses trying to calm them. I was struggling to track my many thoughts, but one of them was, *Oh good, doctors and nurses are here, they will know what to do.*

One woman was banging her head against the wall in a rhythm while wailing loudly. Another was leaning over a trash can heaving and vomiting. One person was wildly swinging her arms in the air as if trying to punch the grief away. Some people were groaning, some were screaming at the top of their lungs and hyperventilating—it was a sheer onslaught of volume and guttural sounds that are indescribable. The experienced chaplains later told me this is known as "wailing and flailing." The family's matriarch had suddenly died on the surgery table from complications, and the nurses brought the family into the Death Room to give them the news. I turned up about three minutes later. Within moments all the white coats were gone, and I was alone with this wailing and flailing family. It turned out that the white coats had thought to themselves, *At least the chaplain is here; he'll know what to do.* No one chooses to be in a situation like this, but this was my job. I was supposed to do something.

I stood there for a couple of minutes trying to tell myself that this was real life, it was time to act. Should I call a coroner? Should I usher the family into the ICU to see their mother? This would be my first-ever time being in the same room as a dead body. What if I passed out or threw up? Should I make funeral arrangements or did someone else? I had no idea, but I was getting very anxious just standing there in the middle of all this volume and commotion.

A leader can only handle the internal and external pressure to do something for so long. I could see the other families in the waiting lounge staring at me. All the noise from the Death Room was escalating their own anxiety, because they all had loved ones in the ICU fighting for their lives. I could feel the nurse who managed the waiting lounge desk looking at me—she didn't want a noisy room. Everyone was anxious, including the young chaplain.

I attempted to talk to this grieving family. "Could someone tell me what happened?"

No response, no acknowledgment that I was even in the room. I walked closer to the hysterical woman and caught one of her swinging fists in my hand. I held it tightly and looked right into her eyes, trying to silently communicate that I cared. She settled down and I asked one of the family members to hold her hand as I worked my way to the lady hitting the wall with her head. I didn't speak, I just took her shoulders and guided her to a seat. This seemed to be working pretty well. Okay, this must be what you do. Take charge. Be kind, but directive. These people were so upset they were barely able to function, let alone communicate. But as I walked over and made eye contact and reached out to touch them, they seemed to calm one at a time. *I can do this*, I thought.

A nurse walked in and beckoned me outside to talk. "Chaplain, we need the bed for another patient. Can you get this family to come visit their mum so we can turn the room?"

So that must be what I was supposed to do—hustle a grieving family in and out to free up needed bed space. It didn't seem very compassionate, but at least I had a clear directive. I walked back in and asserted myself, "It's time to go visit your mother." But this announcement caused a huge regression and reactivated the wailing and flailing. We were back to square one.

At this point you may be thinking, gentle reader, that the chaplain staff had ill-equipped me for this particular moment, and you may be harboring some level of anger toward Randy, the supervisor, with his lack of advice when the pager first went off. I can relate. Why didn't Randy tell me what to do? How irresponsible is a hospital to entrust the care of a family in shock to an inexperienced ministry student?

But Randy knew something I didn't know: no one can prepare you for this. There is no manual, there is no procedure. Leadership in the face of unhinged grief is pure intuition. All you can do is face it, manage yourself, and respond as situations arise.

Standing in that Death Room, I didn't know what I know now. Grief is a tornado. It shows up unexpectedly, it wreaks havoc, and it overstays its welcome. The tornado was churning in this room and all

I had to ward off the storm was an umbrella. My mistake was think-ing I could control *any* aspect of the situation.

But I also realized that I get very anxious when I don't know what to do, because I spent most of my childhood thinking I was stupid, and any time I don't know what to do—even to this day—I feel stupid. When I feel stupid I feel exposed, as if everyone around me knows I'm stupid. I also tend to obligate myself to people I barely know because I'm a chronic people pleaser. So when the nurse came in and pressured me to get the family into the unit, it hit two of my core issues: feeling stupid and pleasing a stranger. I suddenly felt relief that I had a direction and also felt obligated to do what the nurse wanted rather than what the family needed. I didn't know at the time that I hide my insecurity with certainty and confidence, that I'm prone to speak in absolutes even when I'm not sure, and that I have a deep need to be impressive.

But Randy and the clinical pastoral education experience knew all of that. Well, to be fair, they didn't know all of that about me, they simply knew that if they put a person who was open to learning in a trauma environment for a year and helped that person process how she or he showed up, that person would develop self-awareness and become a powerful pastoral presence in the face of massive grief and anxiety. It took me several weeks of dealing with grieving people full time to realize that almost all the time I spoke, it was to quell my own anxiety, not to serve others. Once I was able to name and manage the internal and external pressure to "do something," I could enter a room and pay attention to what that family actually needed.

The year I served as a chaplain I attended more than 250 deaths. I sat with cancer patients, trauma patients, burn victims, and I held stillborn babies. I walked into rooms of high emotion, open hostil-ity, and also rooms of detached indifference. I faced a gang fight in the emergency room waiting lounge, people who smelled putrid, chronically homeless people, mentally unstable people, and violent people. I sat with a man full of shotgun pellets as he died. He had abused his wife for the last time, and she shot him, reloaded, and shot him again. I ministered to terrified parents of very sick young kids and prison transfers who were handcuffed to the gurney. I met with angry, exhausted, and grieving staff. I walked alongside people being rolled into a room, heads strapped down, wide eyes looking up at me, wondering if they'd make it.

A trauma hospital is a microcosm of the human experience, and I experienced all of it. I had no idea at the time how deeply impactful a year of trauma and death would be on my leadership capacity. So much came out of me that I didn't know was in me. I was more human than I could ever admit in Bible college: I was more fearful, doubtful, and less impressive. Under the surface of my cheerful, competent veneer was a shadow that blocked my capacity to serve people and offer true incarnational presence.

That was twenty-two years ago. Since then I have discovered that all of these dynamics show up in *every* leadership context, not just something as extreme as a trauma hospital. Leadership is vulnerable; it exposes a leader's blind spot and his shadow. A leader who wants to grow in self-awareness does not need a trauma context like a hospital, because all leadership puts pressure on a leader and reveals the gap a leader must manage. We all bring more than we realize into our context, and it has more effect than we appreciate.

I was surprised to learn that paying attention to what is going on under the surface is also an effective spiritual growth tool. After following Jesus for about a decade, I became stunted in my spiritual growth because I had thought that growth came from prayer and Bible study. I didn't know that the "boiling collective" always bubbled under the surface, demanding my subconscious focus and blocking my spiritual growth. But after ten years and a professional Bible degree, one more Bible study was not going to do the trick. By paying attention to what was bubbling underneath and managing it,

I discovered new levels of freedom and a profound encounter with God's grace. I experienced genuine spiritual breakthroughs of patterns that had previously kept me stuck.

When we are under pressure, tired, anxious, or feeling threatened, our tendency is to depend on ourselves rather than on God. This is because our "self" is somewhat tangible whereas God is invisible and can feel intangible. I think this is why Jesus, Paul, and the authors of Scripture talk so much about denying self and the dangers of the flesh. But the good news is that I don't have to depend on myself anymore. Jesus has now freed me from the tyranny of anxiety and freed me from having to cover what is happening under the surface. Thanks to grace, I am able to lead out of that depth rather than from a place of anxiety. This is no small thing and is an absolutely delightful side effect of doing this work.

Of course, none of us lead in a vacuum. Part of what makes leadership so fluid is the people we lead, who have their own boiling collective just under the surface like we do. Also, most of us lead more than one person at a time, so our team or family creates a dynamic or a "system" that we also encounter. Effective leadership involves not only self-awareness, but group-awareness and other-awareness—the ability to pay attention to the dynamic of human systems. No wonder leadership can be grueling. There is a lot going on!

We awaken to relational dynamics by studying family systems theory, founded by Murray Bowen in the 1950s. The chaplain in charge of our department, George, had studied directly under Murray Bowen and was a fellow student with Edwin Friedman. Friedman practiced family systems for years as a therapist before adapting Bowen theory to congregations, organizations, and ultimately to leadership in his magnum opus *A Failure of Nerve*.

George, the chaplain supervisor, pushed us to read systems theory and everything his fellow student, Friedman, had written. We learned to attend to not only *content* but also *process* when dealing with patients and their families. Not just what people are saying but *how people are relating*. I learned how to walk into a room and notice the system that was taking place. Who is the secret keeper? Who is the black sheep? Who takes over when a decision has to be made? Who waits to be called on and then complains that he's never given a voice in important decisions? Any group of people, whether it is a family or a staff, takes on relational patterns and becomes a system.

Many times I would walk into a room only to be beckoned out by a family member who wanted to tell me a secret about the person in the bed and his or her illness. A family member would ask me to side against another family member or would disparage a doctor until she walked into the room and then heap praise on her. These dynamics are not limited to a hospital. I could very well be describing your last staff meeting. Or Thanksgiving dinner. That's because according to Bowen and many who have developed family systems theory, any group of people organizes into a system and that system can become chronically anxious over time. Regardless of the group being a nuclear family, staffed employees, a missions group, or a congregation, if it is a group of people, it becomes a dynamic system, each person affecting the other and the whole.

If you can learn some family systems theory, you can lead in an entirely different gear than you're leading in now. You'll not neglect content, *what is being said*, but you'll add the ability to pay attention to process, *how people are relating*, and perhaps most powerfully, *how they are affecting your own anxiety*. Who is quiet all the time? Who takes all the energy in the room? Who needs the last word? Who is passive-aggressive? Who always has a "meeting after the meeting"? Who acts different depending on who is in the room? And most powerfully, what or who is stuck in a predictable pattern?

These are all process issues that a leader can learn to navigate. Once you get the hang of it, you'll find yourself becoming a sociologist of your own self and team—you'll be paying attention to yourself, the system, and what is being said all at the same time. If you really catch on to this approach, you'll help your team do the same. The healthiest teams are not the ones where only the leader is fully aware of these internal and external dynamics, they are the teams where the leader has equipped the entire team to be aware and to communicate freely with one another about them.

Creating an emotionally healthy culture for your people can help their spiritual growth. No one has to pretend anymore or hide or blame when he makes a mistake. No one has to carry shame anymore or get defensive or hold private meetings about someone else. No one has to tiptoe around your shadow and issues—people can openly discuss them with you because you are less reactive and can handle difficult conversations about personal things. You no longer have to hide your own dark side. You can create an openly healthy system for people to thrive.

This is easy to write but difficult to live, and it takes some practice and effort. The stakes are high. Our world has so few leaders who know how to create a healthy culture in their organizations, churches, and even families. But if you're willing to do some personal work to notice what is bubbling under the surface, and if you can develop a family-systems muscle, your spiritual life and therefore your leadership can exponentially grow.

People who are motivated to not only think about the way they think, but courageously walk down new pathways can experience connection with God in a deeper way. They can walk farther by faith because they are no longer being managed by their unconscious reactions.

This whole journey began for me in that intensive care waiting lounge. I spent almost three hours with that family and came away thinking I could never be an effective chaplain. For most of that encounter I felt utterly unskilled for the task at hand. Most leaders wonder if they really are the right person to lead, especially in the early years. I later presented this first encounter to our group of residents and supervisors using a tool called a verbatim. I gave myself a solid F for my efforts. I felt that I must be an imposter, the wrong person to do the job, but the experienced supervisors were much more gracious with me.

They explained that no amount of experience equips you to manage the wailing and flailing visits. You just get through them, and you almost always give yourself a failing grade. And so it is with some leadership encounters. No matter how much you train, you're going to lose a few, you're going to get it wrong, or you might lead your team down a path that ends in a brick wall of defeat. Even when you do it well, you'll grade yourself poorly. This material will not guarantee positive outcomes. You will lose a few positive outcomes. You will continue to deal with difficult people and unknown situations. But this material will forge a path through any leaderships scenario so you can get through to the other side. An essential part of our leadership journey is being kind to ourselves as we navigate these challenges. We all make mistakes, we all feel like imposters from time to time, but all of us can start by paying attention to how we show up and what triggers us. We all have the capacity to bravely die to our weaknesses and discover life on the other side of our assumptions, fears, and anxieties.

DISCUSSION QUESTIONS

1. Talk about an early leadership role you had that you felt ill-equipped to navigate. What was the role and why did you feel ill-equipped?
2. Can you think of a time recently when you didn't know what to do, but had to do something? What was that like for you? Can you name the pressures you were feeling, internally or externally?

3. Think of a time in your life when you led but gave yourself a low grade for your efforts. What happened?

4. Have you ever stepped on a "leadership land mine"—you're leading a group and someone blows up because of something you said or did, but you didn't see it coming?

5. Name a relational dynamic that has you confused or frustrated. It may be an employee or a family member, but it is a recurring pattern of behavior between you and this person that is getting nowhere.

two

ANXIETY, FREEDOM, AND HOW THE GOSPEL WORKS

The more a man dies to himself, the more he begins to live unto God.
—THOMAS À KEMPIS

The goal of managing anxiety is not simply for relief, it is to connect more fully with God and to raise awareness of what God is doing. Anxiety blocks our awareness of God because it takes our subconscious attention. This means that anxiety can be an early detection system that we're depending on something other than God for our well-being. Of course, not all anxiety is a sign that we're off base. If your child is playing on the highway and you're anxious about it, that is a sign to act, not pause and consider what might be blocking God. But in many leadership and relational situations, anxiety is a warning sign that something is getting in the way of your well-being. What exactly is getting in the way? Anxiety is a signal, not a root cause. It is a siren that a storm might be coming; it is not the storm itself. Getting to the root cause is key to transformation and systemic health.

I believe leadership anxiety is generated when we think we need something in any particular moment that we don't actually need. When I began as a hospital chaplain, I would get anxious walking into a room because I believed I needed to know what to say or what to do. As much as I believed I needed that, it wasn't true. As I progressed in my awareness, I was able to walk into a room not knowing what to say, not even knowing what I was walking into, because there was a larger truth at work beyond what I believed. I believed I needed knowledge to be okay; I believed I was required to say just the right thing to make things better. As I dug in deeper, I later learned that I believed I had to appear smart to be okay, so when I didn't know what to say, I was managing my own feeling of inadequacy rather than connecting with the people in the room.

The greater truth was that God was present in those situations; God was in the room before I walked in, and God would guide me. I did not, in fact, need to know what to say. The more I depended on needing to say the right thing, the less effective I was as a chaplain. I was managing my own anxiety rather than paying attention to God. What is this dynamic, and why did I believe I needed it so strongly? Of course, I write in the past tense, but I still get anxious today in leadership contexts, and much of the time it is because the situation is putting pressure on what I think I need that I do not actually need. The situation is also blocking my capacity to notice and trust God in those moments.

Anxiety shrinks the power of the gospel because it presents a false gospel—one of self-reliance rather than reliance on God. The gospel of self-reliance is always bad news because it always leads to more anxiety. But if I can learn to notice it, eventually name its source and triggers, and move past it, I encounter the actual good news of Jesus, the gospel of grace, which always leads to freedom. The consistent witness of the New Testament is that freedom and life come when we deny, crucify, and are wary of something inside us that shrinks the gospel. What is it inside us that gets in the way?

In the original Greek language, Jesus talked about denying the *autos* or the "self." "Whoever wants to be my disciple must deny themselves [autos] and take up their cross and follow me" (Matt. 16:24). When Paul wrote about this same topic, he didn't talk much about the *autos*. His preferred descriptors were *anthropos* and *sarx*, which are translated "man" and "flesh." Even though Paul used different words, I believe he was speaking about the same concept. Paul challenged us to beware of the power *anthropos* and *sarx* can have over us. Here are some brief examples. I have added the Greek word to each text for emphasis:

Those who belong to Christ Jesus have crucified the flesh [*sarx*] with its passions and desires. (Gal. 5:24)

You, my brothers and sisters, were called to be free. But do not use your freedom to indulge the flesh [*sarx*]; rather, serve one another humbly in love. (Gal. 5:13)

For I know that good itself does not dwell in me, that is, in my sinful nature [*sarx*]. (Rom. 7:18)

You were taught, with regard to your former way of life, to put off your old self [*anthropos*], which is being corrupted by its deceitful desires; to be made new in the attitude of your minds; and to put on the new self, created to be like God in true righteousness and holiness. (Eph. 4:22–24)

I count at least twenty-six occasions in the New Testament where
freedom and life are the promised outcomes from denying, crucify-
ing, and watching out for the *autos, sarx,* or *anthropos.* Greek studies
can be risky endeavors because the words are more fluid than we
like. Each of the words above are also used in positive contexts in the
New Testament. For example, one of the most beautiful passages of
Scripture was written by John: "The Word became flesh [*sarx*] and
made his dwelling among us." (John 1:14).

Not every use of those Greek words is negative, and we could
spend a whole chapter diving into the context of each word. Instead
I propose that each time Jesus and Paul invited us to deny, crucify,
and be wary of this "thing," it was to free us so we could encounter
the true gospel. This "thing" is something we think we need in the
moment, and when we do not get it, we become very anxious. This
anxiety blocks our awareness of God, makes us believe a lie, and keeps
us from encountering grace. It teaches us a false gospel—that we need
something other than Christ in any given moment to be okay. I think
this is why so many people get stuck in their spiritual growth, because
they never wrestle with what this thing is, when it shows up and what
triggers it. Instead of denying it or dying to it, they entrench it.

Thomas Merton called this thing the "false self." He wrote,
"Every one of us is shadowed by an illusory person: a false self. We are
not very good at recognizing illusions, least of all the ones we cherish
about ourselves—the ones we are born with and which feed the roots
of sin. For most of the people in the world, there is no greater subjec-
tive reality than this false self of theirs. A life devoted to the cult of
this shadow is what is called a life of sin."[1]

Leadership anxiety is generated by this false self. Anxiety is a
sign that the false self is demanding we nourish it instead of dying to
it. The false self blocks us from receiving the gospel in all its power
and beauty. It keeps us stuck in recurring patterns and does not
bring about true freedom and life. James Finley was an apprentice

of Thomas Merton and wrote much about the theology of false self. He wrote, "In our zeal to become the landlords of our own being, we cling to each achievement as a kind of verification of our self-proclaimed reality. We become the center and God somehow recedes to an invisible fringe."[2]

When we are under pressure, feeling threatened or anxious, we depend on this false self rather than depending on God. If we can learn to notice when it is at play, name what we think we need that we do not actually need, and then die to it, we can be freed from its grip and opened to a deeper experience of grace. I am not talking about heaven and hell and the forgiveness of sins or a transaction with God in the past. I am talking about freedom and transformation moment by moment. I think this is one reason Jesus calls us to deny it daily. Sometimes we need to deny it hourly or moment by moment to encounter God's freedom. In this approach, anxiety becomes a gift rather than a curse because it serves as an early detection device that your false self is at work. Let's take one example from Paul as to how we can break free from the false self.

THE POWER OF THE GOSPEL VERSUS THE FALSE SELF

When I first became a follower of Jesus in the 1980s, I thought the good news was all about the future: eternal life after I die. But as I've studied Scripture, and the teachings of Jesus and Paul in particular, I've discovered that the gospel has power available to help me in the present and even in my past: eternal life right now. Paul's letter to the Romans is a stunning, complex explanation of the gospel. In chapter 6 of the letter, he explains how the power of the gospel helps us in the present. Paul shows us how to access this good news moment by moment and why dying to self is such a freeing way to live.

For we know that our old self [*anthropos*] was crucified with him so that the body ruled by sin might be done away with, that we should no longer be slaves to sin—because anyone who has died has been set free from sin. . . . The death he died, he died to sin once for all; but the life he lives, he lives to God. In the same way, count yourselves dead to sin but alive to God in Christ Jesus. Therefore do not let sin reign in your mortal body so that you obey its evil desires. Do not offer any part of yourself to sin as an instrument of wickedness, but rather offer yourselves to God as those who have been brought from death to life; and offer every part of yourself to him as an instrument of righteousness. For sin shall no longer be your master, because you are not under the law, but under grace. (Rom. 6:6–7, 10–14)

Paul explains what was lost on me for years: we can simultaneously be free from the power of sin, yet still struggle with sin. Christ's death has conquered sin's power, but somehow sin still invites us in. When Paul talks about sin in Romans, he is almost always talking about a noun, not a verb. In Romans, Paul describes sin as a condition you are in, not something you do. There are two Greek words for sin: the noun *hamartia*, and the verb *hamartanō*. In Romans, Paul uses the noun forty-six times and the verb twice. So for Paul, being set free from sin is more about a condition you are in rather than things you do. It is about being infected and then healed rather than doing wrong things. In fact, in Romans 1, the "bad things" we do are a symptom of the condition of sin, rather than the sin itself.

Why do I still sin when I have been set free from sin? Paul explains that it all comes down to where we offer our energy and time. Paul is implying that sin gains power over us the more we engage in it. But so does God, so it all comes down to where we give our energy and time. I think Paul's principle states: *where we put our attention defines our spiritual growth.* If we make a habit of offering ourselves to sin, then sin becomes our master—it gains power and control over our lives—but if we habitually offer ourselves to God, his power takes over and frees us from sin's grip. Whatever we give ourselves to is what has our attention and devotion.

I think this is why Paul said we can either be a slave to sin or a slave to God. Some might say, "If my only two choices involve being a slave to something, then forgot it." These thinkers fundamentally misunderstand the way the world works. We are all a slave to something or someone. We all give ourselves to something or someone. As a result, whatever we give ourselves to becomes our master. Some of our favorite stories show this to be true. Gollum in *The Lord of the Rings* is slowly consumed by what he reaches for until he becomes less and less human. Walter White, the protagonist/antagonist in *Breaking Bad*, slowly becomes more evil as he gives himself over to evil enterprises. Paul said we ought to proceed with extreme caution when offering ourselves to something or someone, because if we choose anything other than God, it puts us on a path of death. Paul explicitly reminds us a little further in this same chapter that "the wages of sin is death, but the gift of God is eternal life" (Rom. 6:23).

Sin kills. God gives life.

I think for too many years we have mistakenly taught that God kills and God gives life, but that is not what Paul taught. Paul wasn't saying that God punishes us when we sin, he was saying that *sin punishes us when we sin.* The reason to not live in sin isn't so much about disappointing God or angering God; the reason to avoid sin at all costs is to avoid sin's price, which is always death. Sometimes sin causes literal death, but most often it kills something we love—a relationship, our integrity, our ability to look someone in the eyes. Sin is always on the prowl looking to destroy. God is always in the life-giving business. We have a choice all the time: give ourselves to sin, which destroys, or give ourselves to God, who gives life.

So, what about Paul's statement that Christ broke the *power* of sin? What does that look like? When I was younger, I had a compulsive need for people to think I was funny. Sometimes if I was trying to be funny in a group and everyone would laugh except one person, then I'd make that person the brunt of my humor to the point that a couple of times the person left the group in tears. I needed to do that because I needed the attention—without that laughter, I was not okay. The next day or even hours after I had made the person the brunt of my humor, I would feel terrible that I had caused pain for someone; but in the moment, I was in such need of the attention that I lost all reason. At the time, I was not vulnerable enough or mature enough to go back to that group and apologize, so I had to cover my shame the next time I was around those people. I tried to be extra nice to the person I had mocked, for example.

There was something very dark in me that needed that affirmation, even at the cost of another person. But that behavior always led to death. Every. Single. Time. Death of my own freedom, death of a healthy relationship, death of my reputation. It also led to punishment—self-loathing after I had done it, the extra burden of trying too hard the next time, and so forth. That's how I knew it was sin—when I gave myself to it, there was no life in it, only death. Even when I got the laugh from the group, the feeling of affirmation was fleeting. You could say the "life" of that laugh never lasted. That's because the source of that laugh was not everlasting life; it was death. Making people laugh is not sin, of course. The sin is needing to make people laugh at any cost to be okay.

Sin, death, exhaustion, shame, and anxiety are bred from being a slave to the wrong thing. As I continued to give myself to this need, it consumed me. Even when I thought I had satisfaction, it never lasted. Making people laugh as a teen might sound innocuous, but this exact dynamic is at play with someone fighting for sobriety. Ask anyone with a recovery chip in his pocket, and he will tell you this same story. The consequences may be more dire, but the internal dynamic of feeding what we think we need to be okay is the same.

Christ's death freed me from needing approval from the group, and it is no small freedom. The power that had me in its grip is forever overpowered by Jesus. There is now a greater power than the power of sin. All the things I used to need to be okay, such as the need to win over a group and to be the smartest person in the room and to always be right. Before I had Christ in my life, I needed validation at any cost, and when I got it, my need was never satiated, it only increased. But Christ's death broke the power of that need in me.

I still want affirmation today and I am still very much a people pleaser; thus I still struggle with sin, but its power is deflated. Before Christ I *had* to have it. Now Christ is my primary need. He fulfills the need for validation, by his grace, in a way that nothing else can compare. My identity, my need to be okay, is found in the grace of Christ. I am freed from hunting for worth at all costs outside of Christ. I am now happily a "slave" to Christ, and the more I give myself to him, the more clearly I see the path of death I was on and the more life-giving my relationships are. Paul was saying that now that we are in Christ, the jig is up with sin; it no longer has power over us because Christ has pulled back the curtain and shown its false allure.

I see Romans 6 as a fork in the road, and every day I get to choose which path I will walk. Before, I blindly followed my own desires down a path and ended up burned and burning others. Now by grace Christ has shown me the end of that road and invites me down a better, more life-giving path. Whatever we offer ourselves to will consume us. I didn't know before how desperately I needed approval—it had tremendous power over me, power enough for me to hurt someone to get it. But now I see that power for what it is, so I choose life-giving power instead. That path looks like a blue flame to a moth; if I chase after it, I'll get scorched.

The miracle of salvation isn't that Jesus stops us from sinning or being tempted to sin, it is that Jesus changes what our hearts want. I still struggle with the same sins as before, but what I want has miraculously changed. I want Christ and lasting life, rather than the fleeting high of attention. The validation I craved from others is Merton's false self and the New Testament's *autos, anthropos,* and *sarx.*

At this point you may be feeling a sense of whiplash from the previous chapter. We went from an anxious hospital encounter to a deep dive into Paul's theology of sin and self, but this is foundational to our later study of anxiety—how it works and how it gets hold of us. We will examine the source of anxiety. We will notice and name it so we can deny it and rest free in Christ. This is how denying self actually works. We notice our anxiety, we prayerfully name its source to God, and we rest free in our identity in Christ and his work instead of what we think we need. We can argue whether anxiety is technically sin or not, but that is hardly the point. The point is that anxiety becomes a marker that something other than my identity in Christ is at play: a false self that leads to death, not life.

> *The miracle of salvation isn't that Jesus stops us from sinning or being tempted to sin, it is that Jesus changes what our hearts want.*

I find this to be incredibly good news because it means that the power of the gospel is available to me anytime. When I am anxious or tired or under threat, I tend to forget the gospel power because I am resorting to what I think I need that I don't really need. If we remove the baggage around the word *sin* and simply see it as a description of something that damages and binds us, then we can use Paul's teaching to help remove the grip of anxiety in our lives.

I will often use the phrase in this book, *Easier written than done!* Even after knowing and practicing this for some years, I still relapse regularly.

Some of you might be perfectionists who have a strong internal critic. Those of you who are particularly hard on yourselves will face an added challenge: In the early months of awareness, you will relapse more than not. You will face an added temptation to condemn yourself by saying, "I should know better by now." Have some self-compassion. You have become aware of your anxiety triggers but haven't yet built enough muscle to intervene. Saying "I should know better by now" is simply an extra layer of death and condemnation. This principle will take time and practice to take effect in your life, which means you will fail a lot before succeeding. I would encourage you to have Romans 8:1–2 at the ready for those moments: "Therefore, there is now no condemnation for those who are in Christ Jesus, because through Christ Jesus the law of the Spirit who gives life has set you free from the law of sin and death."

So yes, it can take years and many walks down the path toward death before we change our ways, but once we experience our heart changing what it wants, we will walk the sinful path less because we will be hungry for life, not destruction. We will also be ruined for the sinful path because we've seen the end so much more clearly and we've seen the pettiness of what we thought we needed, and we've drunk deeper in the grace of God. One effective tool that has helped drive this home for me is a simple prayer I frequently offer to God: *Jesus died so I don't have to _____ anymore.*

For each of us, the blank is different. For me, it is usually some variation of, "Jesus died so I don't have to seek people's approval anymore" or "Jesus died so every sermon does not have to be gold standard anymore."

"Jesus died so I no longer have to make people laugh anymore." And hey, don't get me wrong, I'm still a hilarious guy, but I'm no longer a slave to laughter. I no longer need to use humor to be okay. Now I am freed to use humor to serve people. In the interest of full disclosure, some of my staff and all my children would read this last sentence and say, "Actually, sometimes he uses humor for his own enjoyment. We don't find it funny, but he makes us sit through it." Fair enough, but I no longer use it to damage someone.

Paul is getting right to the heart of what matters most in these middle chapters of Romans. We can keep propping up the false self, but it will never ever lead to life. It only leads to exhaustion and anxiety. God has forged a new path in Jesus that leads to life and freedom. Walking by faith, then, is the lifelong habit of trusting God's story over the story we tell ourselves. Contemplate this modified phrase: *Jesus died to free me from needing* _____ *anymore.* This simple prayer can help dislodge us off one path and connect us into God's path of freedom. On this path, the power and scope of the gospel significantly expands for us, and stopping to pray is a simple, tangible way to change paths. Eugene Peterson said, "Prayer is the way we work our way out of the comfortable but cramped world of self and into the spacious world of God."[3]

If you are a leader, the final benefit of noticing anxiety and dying to the false self is growing in your capacity to be fully present to people. You can lead with humility—not thinking less of yourself, but thinking about yourself less. By doing this, you become less self-absorbed. Anxiety exacts a toll and bolsters self, but noticing it and naming it allows us to be others-focused.

MORE FALSE ANXIETY: FOLLOWING JESUS VERSUS BECOMING LIKE JESUS

I thought grace got you in the door and then
after that you have to prove yourself.
—NEPHTALI MATTA

For most of my Christian life, I thought my job was to strive to become like Christ, but the effort to become like Christ is just another path of anxiety and death.

Wait, what? Trying to become like Jesus is a path of anxiety and death? Aren't we supposed to strive to be like Jesus?

No. I can never, ever become like Jesus.

At a recent men's retreat, our men divided into two groups to play a game. The first group had to identify who among them had attended the most church services in their life. The second group made a list of all the things that Jesus can do that we cannot do. Yeah . . . okay . . . when I said we did this to play a game, I'm realizing just how nerdy I'm making our men's retreat sound, so let me add: we also had a marksmanship contest and played golf.

So, the first group—the person who had attended the most church services was Johnny, a retired pastor. He had attended more than eleven thousand services. We asked Johnny a simple question: "For those eleven thousand church services, in how many of them did the preacher get someone on stage and congratulate them for being like Jesus?" None. After attending more than eleven thousand church services, Johnny had never witnessed a single time when a church leader noticed another person in church and said, "You've made it; you're just like Jesus. Well done." If the goal is to mimic Christ, don't you think one of us should have accomplished that by now? Or maybe you're thinking, *Well, the goal isn't to arrive, it is to strive toward it.* Really? To dangle an unreachable carrot beyond people? That seems cruel to me, a way for good people to give up on following Jesus altogether.

Greyhound racing was a thing where I grew up. I know almost nothing about dog racing, I just know that the dogs wear muzzles to keep them from biting each other, they're skinny, and they run really fast. They also chase a rabbit. The dogs are loaded into a chute, each in their own gated lane, and then at the signal, the gates open and a rabbit magically appears out of nowhere for them to chase. The greyhounds see the rabbit and run as fast as they can, chasing it around the track. Owners and onlookers bet millions of dollars hoping one particular dog will be the fastest at chasing the rabbit. Except that rabbit isn't real. For thousands of races each year, everything goes along without a hitch, the dogs wait in the chute, the fake metal rabbit comes around the track, and when the rabbit is within sight but out of reach of the dogs, the gates open and the dogs start running. They cross the finish line without ever catching the rabbit.

There are at least two recorded occasions when things didn't go as planned. The first incident happened at Shepparton Raceway in Victoria, Australia. The dogs were racing beautifully, fake rabbit just out of reach, when a live, fur-and-all rabbit ran across the track in front of the greyhounds. The greyhound running in third place was hankering for a taste of bunny and immediately changed targets. Instead of chasing the fake rabbit, he went after the real thing. That live rabbit, also known as the world's luckiest rabbit with massive timing issues, managed to get away unscathed, but at least the greyhound had the sense to spot the real thing. The second incident happened at Bendigo Raceway, also in Victoria. The dogs were about thirty seconds into the race when the metal rabbit had a power failure and slowed down. The first dog ran right past it, then figured out the rabbit was behind him and circled back. The rest of the dogs gathered around the fake rabbit, pushing on it with their muzzled mouths, trying to get a bite. What happened next was extraordinary: the dogs started to play. They were prancing around with tails high in the air, some even wagging. They were like puppies, all having a good time around that fake rabbit. They had given up the chase and were enjoying themselves instead of working so hard.

I know what that feels like. I have been a follower of Christ for more than three decades—most of my teenage life and all my adult life. About fifteen years ago I gave up the chase to mimic Christ because I discovered that the rabbit of mimicking Christ was constantly out of reach. Most important, it wasn't real. The rabbit isn't Jesus. Jesus is real. The rabbit is the unattainable quest to mimic Christ, to become like Christ in this lifetime. Jesus does not call us to mimic him but to manifest him. The difference between trying to be like Jesus and simply following Jesus is life changing.

Too much of our church language subtly and overtly sends us the message that our job as followers of Jesus is to become like Jesus. We even quote the Bible sometimes. But it is a false rabbit not worth chasing. Our work isn't to try to become like Jesus. Our work is more difficult than that, it is more fruitful and freeing. Our work is to die to self. There is a canyon-sized gap between trying to become like Jesus and dying to self. One leads to legalism, bondage, and exhaustion; the other leads to the freedom offered by Jesus. You may be thinking, *Wait just a hot minute there, I'm pretty sure the authors of Scripture talked about becoming like Christ.* Yes they did. And every time they did, they described it using the passive voice. Here is one quick example from Paul to the churches in Galatia: "My dear children, for whom I am again in the pains of childbirth until Christ is formed in you" (Gal. 4:19).

Christ *formed in* you.

Becoming like Christ is what God does in us, not what we do. God is the active agent; we are the recipient. The spiritual transformation is God's work. What is our work then? Does God do all the work and we just sit around in life's hot tub, lazily waiting? No, we have work to do as well, it just isn't trying to become like Christ. It is equally hard work, perhaps more difficult than the attempt to be like Jesus. Having died to our false self, our flesh, God now performs his resurrection miracle in us. We are now in a posture to be resurrected by the power of God into the freedom of life in God. It's not about shirking responsibility, it is about a clear division of labor. Our job: die to false self. God's job: transform us into the likeness of Christ.

When we try to become like Christ on our own, we end up back on the path of death. We use a religious good, the well-meaning attempt to become like Jesus, for a more sophisticated version of legalism. Wasn't the very first temptation to humans the offer to become like God? Look where that ended up. Jesus said it clearly, "Whoever wants to be my disciple must deny themselves and take up their cross and follow me" (Matt. 16:24). And Paul wrote: "I have been crucified with Christ and I no longer live, but Christ lives in me. The life I now live in the body, I live by faith in the Son of God, who loved me and gave himself for me" (Gal. 2:20).

The second group at our men's retreat had a different task than the first. Their task was to list all the things Jesus could do that we will never be able to do. Here is a partial list: feed five thousand people with a kid's snack, walk on water, tell a storm to calm down, raise someone from the dead, raise himself from the dead, be tempted but never sin, know the right thing to do and say in every situation, perfectly love and welcome all kinds of people, die for our sins. The list is what makes Jesus utterly distinct from us. No matter how hard we try, we are incapable of doing those things. They are exclusively in Jesus' realm because he is God and we will never be God. The list is actually the reason we *worship* Jesus. Stop expending energy trying to become like Christ; instead, put your energy into dying to self and following and worshipping Christ, which is what God has been calling us to do all along. You will never be like Jesus, but you can become a healthier follower of Jesus. Anyone has what it takes to follow God and worship God, but none of us can become like God, and that should be the best news you've heard in years.

And hey, if you're struggling with this idea, think of it this way: which of Jesus' apostles do you think was most like Jesus? They were all very different types of people and were, quite frankly, nothing like Jesus in many ways, yet they were all incredible followers of Jesus. Or to push the idea to an absurd point, we *all* have distinct personalities. Some of us have taken various personality tests—Enneagram, Myers-Briggs, DiSC profile, StrengthsFinder. But Jesus had a personality too—probably different from yours. Imagine spending a lifetime of effort to become like Christ but finding out that you are an ENTJ and he was an INFP, or you are an Enneagram type 8 and Jesus was an Enneagram . . . what . . . all nine numbers? How does that work with God? Just when you thought you could be like Christ, you realize you're not because you are wired different from Jesus! I am being facetious here, but it exposes a very real problem: when we talk about being like Christ, we forget that he is utterly distinct from us. In our effort to become like him, we actually fall into a sophisticated form of idolatry—we tend to make Jesus into a perfected version of our image and then strive to become like that. Nope. We will never be like Christ. Let's deny false self, worship him, and be free.

ANOTHER SOURCE OF THEOLOGICAL ANXIETY: OUR GIFTS AND THEIR SHADOW SIDE

What you focus on determines what you miss.
—IAN CRON

The charismatic, type A leader is proud and arrogant. The quiet, come-alongside leader is afraid to step up and take charge. The gifted speaker talks too much. The hospitable person judges the decor of others. The perfectionist does everything with excellence but has low output because she only does what she can manage perfectly. Every human being is gifted by God to serve for God's glory, but every gift has a shadow side that can take over if left unchecked.

I tend to think out loud and can have the rather annoying habit of switching my point of view as I'm speaking. I also sound confident in what I'm saying, even when I'm not sure of what I am saying. This makes me infuriating to follow sometimes. The positive side of this little collection is that I am naturally entrepreneurial, I am able to run several concurrent options for a decision at any given time, I am highly optimistic, and I am not easily stuck. These very traits have helped our church over the course of my leadership, but the shadow side of those gifts have hindered us as well. You can imagine the challenge this presents to a new staff member, figuring out how to navigate the shadow side of the top leader of the organization.

A few years into leading this church, I was spitballing some ideas with our team, not sure what I thought but trying to discern a direction by talking it through and listening to myself talk. One of our newer staff, who is a concrete thinker and a very diligent person, took out a notepad and earnestly wrote down everything I was saying as if it were a papal edict. I was horrified. The shadow side of my gift was going to cause this excellent team member a whole lot of work because, as the old timers on the team could attest, it was highly likely I wouldn't be leading us in this same direction the following month. I was just talking to figure out what I thought. Because she didn't know me, because I was the boss, and because of her wiring, she was writing it all down as a command to follow. Ever since then I have been much more mindful of how the shadow side of my gifting impacts people. One staff member who has served several years with me often says, "Last month you were talking this way. Are you still thinking we're heading down that direction?" She knows how to mitigate my shadow.

The fruit of true self-awareness is being more present to others.

When I was training for ministry, I misguidedly thought I should work on eliminating my shadow. I refer you to earlier in this chapter—the futile effort to become more like Jesus. I spent an entire year working on my pride and arrogance. The gifting side of my pride and arrogance is my upfront leadership and my ability to lead my team into difficult places. I prayed, worked on it, but I became exasperated at the lack of progress. I have since learned that God has not called us to rid ourselves of the shadow, for we would also rid the gift. Instead God calls us to a much more difficult and nuanced battle: the battle of Romans 6. Offer my gift to God for God's glory or to self for my glory? At the risk of simplifying, will I serve out of my gifting or my shadow? In my life the answer is almost always some combination of both. Every time I walk out to preach, I am faced with my gift and its shadow—which will I offer?

Paul wrote to the churches in Rome, "In view of God's mercy . . . offer your bodies as a living sacrifice, holy and pleasing to God—this is your true and proper worship. Do not conform to the pattern of this world, but be transformed by the renewing of your mind" (Rom. 12:1–2). So, offering ourselves to God and dying is our side of the division of labor, our "living sacrifice." God's part is the miraculous transformation of our minds: our assumptions, our idols, the stories we tell ourselves, and so forth. This is a lifelong and rather frustrating process. Frustrating because once you're aware of it, you soon discover just how much time and energy you spend depending on and strengthening your false self, especially when you are under pressure, anxious, or exhausted (which for a leader is most of the time). Self-awareness isn't self-absorption or self-centeredness, the fruit of true self-awareness is being more present to others.

My shadow side seeks a laugh for myself, but having seen the path to death this becomes, I now am motivated to use that gift for God and for God's people. Can I create a laugh not for self, but for the good of the group? On the surface of things, this can look like a wafer-thin line—both paths involve a group laughing—but in my heart I know the canyon-sized difference between feeding what I think I need and living for God. My gifts still have a shadow, of course. I will never eliminate the shadow. But much like Paul promised, that the power of sin can be broken even though we still struggle with sin, so can the power of the shadow be reduced even though it still exists. So, I still think out loud, change directions, and occasionally exasperate my team, but God has shown me the impact of the shadow; therefore I choose to work on its impact. One of the most effective ways to reduce the impact of a shadow is to talk about it with your team. If your team feels safe, they will be able to tell you the impact of your shadow, and you can tell them theirs. Brace yourself. It is never a comfortable conversation.

THE ONGOING FREEDOM BATTLE

Paul issued a stern warning to the church in Galatia, "It is for freedom that Christ has set us free. Stand firm, then, and do not let yourselves be burdened again by a yoke of slavery" (Gal. 5:1). Paul knew something I think we don't fully grasp; the battle for freedom is an ongoing battle. When I first became a follower of Jesus, I thought it meant I was free forever, no more effort required. Now I know that the power has been broken, yes, but I am in an ongoing battle for freedom.

Jesus told a stark parable about housecleaning, "When an impure spirit comes out of a person, it goes through arid places seeking rest and does not find it. Then it says, 'I will return to the house I left.' When it arrives, it finds the house swept clean and put in order. Then it goes and takes seven other spirits more wicked than itself, and they go in and live there. And the final condition of that person is worse than the first" (Luke 11:24–26). Yowzers! Jesus was warning us that if we're not careful, we can clean up our lives only to be at higher risk for invasion again. I think the battle for freedom works the same way. This is why I think self-awareness alone is overrated. Learning more about ourselves and what is bubbling under the surface is a good thing, but if we stop our learning at that point, all we've done is swept the house clean. So many people are self-aware but still unhealthy. True transformation and therefore deeper experiences of freedom come when we move from self-awareness to dying to self to following Jesus down a new path of freedom. This takes more work than most of us realize at first. Old habits and ways of thinking are deeply entrenched in us, so often it comes down to a battle.

Freedom in God's kingdom has two facets: we are freed *from* and we are freed *to*. In modern Western society, freedom means autonomy. We dangerously believe freedom means, "I can do anything I want." But Scripture authors never describe freedom this way, they describe it like this: "Something used to have hold of me, but a better power released me from it and now that better power has hold of me." We are never free floating, free to do whatever we want, free from control. We are, in fact, always connecting to someone or something. Freed *from* and freed *to*. And this freedom involves an ongoing battle.

When we study the great freedom movements of human history, we see this is true. Moses had to fight for freedom, so did Gandhi and Martin Luther King. Throughout history, the oppressor never willingly hands power over to the oppressed, rather the oppressed have to fight for their freedom. You may have to battle to break free from some deeply entrenched habits and ways of thinking. Christ has set us free, and we are free indeed, but there is another law at work, lurking in the shadows waiting to put me in bondage. In between those forces is my decision: What am I giving myself to today? Am I feeding false self or God? Am I walking down the path that leads to death or the path of life and freedom?

As we learn to pay attention to anxiety, we use it as an early detection system that we are moving into bondage. Before we get too far down that path, we can stop, pray (Jesus died so I don't have to _____ anymore), remember where our identity is found, die to what we think we need in that moment that we don't really need, and experience freedom on the spot. As I will say dozens of times in this book, easier written than done. We will still struggle, still fail, have a shadow, give in to self. We will still be anxious, but none of that will have mastery over us anymore.

For me, the good news of the gospel is that my anxiety no longer has the last word. There is now another word after anxiety has spoken or failure has spoken, and that word is *life*. God speaks life and identity. Anxiety and failure speak death and condemnation. As you explore this for yourself, I would encourage you, as much as you are able, to be as kind to yourself as God is when you fail. And keep walking and keep fighting for freedom. It is well worth the effort.

DISCUSSION QUESTIONS

1. Can you name something you think you need that you don't really need to be okay?
2. How might you begin to notice when you are giving in to that need?
3. Using the prayer, "Jesus died so I don't have to _____ anymore," what are some of the blanks for you?
4. What is your reaction to the idea that Jesus doesn't actually call us to become like him, but rather to die to self, follow and worship him? What does this change for you?
5. What are some of your gifts, and what are some of the shadow sides of those gifts?
6. If you are in a group, would you be willing to discuss these gifts and shadows with one another?

three

SOURCES OF
INTERNAL ANXIETY

When a patient's heart stops beating, first take your own pulse.
—A DOCTOR'S ADVICE TO ME WHILE SERVING
ON THE HOSPITAL CODE TEAM

One of my favorite childhood experiences was deep-sea fishing with my family. My grandad built his own boat and we would stay on it for a week or two every summer. He'd anchor at Narrow Neck, a quiet bay off the back end of Rottnest Island, fourteen miles off the coast of Western Australia. Every morning after breakfast we would go several miles into the open sea to drift fish. We'd spread out around the back of the boat and drop a thick line with heavy weights and large hooks baited with octopus chunks. Our line would plunge down a couple hundred feet and we'd drift over reef and sand. At that depth we had no idea what we might catch, which was the fun of it. We would feel a bite, set the hook, and then pull up the fish to see what we had caught. The top prize was a dhufish, a silver fish with sweet flesh. Red snapper, sweep, queenfish, and breaksea cod were also highly prized table fish. We used every other fish for the lobster pots. It was a grand adventure for a kid.

The problem with deep-sea fishing was the tangles. As I pulled in the fish, I couldn't wind the line back around the huge spool, especially with the weights and the fish tugging against me, so I just had to let the line loop near my feet. I'd haul the fish into the boat and it would lay in the line as I removed the hook and set it into the big bucket.

Unaddressed anxiety blocks effective leadership because a leader gives too much energy to the anxiety rather than to the situation or person at hand.

I'd come back to my spot to find an utter tangle of line, weights, and hooks in a twisted mess. Almost every time we went fishing, I ended up with an overwhelming tangle at my feet. As a result, my grandmother would stop her fishing and come untangle my line for me. She would spend up to an hour patiently untangling the line, getting the weights out of the way, and wrapping it cleanly back on the spool so I could fish again. I marveled at her patience to untangle my line and also how she and Grandad and my parents never seemed to get a tangle. I remember at the time thinking, *That must be what adulthood is: you never get a tangle.*

Anxiety is a tangle of emotions that can be overwhelming to sort through. These emotions manifest in a spinning mind, a racing heart, or a tightened gut. These next chapters are about untangling anxiety by categorizing and naming its sources. Some anxiety is internal, some is relational, and most is a combination of both. By naming or "diagnosing" the source of anxiety, we gain some power over it, and rather than it holding us, we are able to hold it and then give it to God.

The goal is not simply to be free from anxiety's grip, but freed to be more present to God and the people we're called to serve. This is how we live out the "freed from and freed to" nature of God's kingdom. On the other hand, unaddressed anxiety blocks effective leadership because a leader gives too much energy to the anxiety rather than to the situation or person at hand.

One of my friends, Charles, is a worship leader at a local church. He wrote,

> In my job, I've seen firsthand when the team I'm leading has absorbed my own anxiety. Each band member has his or her own obstacles to overcome (stage fright, whether they know their part well enough, clearing out what's swirling around in their head so they can concentrate on the music). When I take the stage without checking my own anxiety, the entire worship set usually suffers. To make matters worse, it's not just that the team takes on my anxiety, there's a room of hundreds of people who have to pay for it, not to mention a preacher taking the stage after a lackluster music experience. Anxiety has a powerful negative impact on my leading, so paying attention to sources is essential for me.

Many people are not aware of their anxiety until it becomes overwhelming. As you pay more attention to your anxiety, you will be able to intervene earlier before it builds steam. The first step of this awareness is noticing your physiology. In my life, anxiety primarily manifests as a spinning mind. My brain can race like a rodent on a wheel, and I have learned over time to pay attention to four signs that require early intervention:

- If I am spending too much time worrying before a meeting, as though obsessively thinking about it will somehow preempt the outcome.

- If I'm having an anger fantasy at someone in my head.
- If the problem is the last thing I think about before sleep and already on my mind when I wake up.
- An inability to focus on one of my kids when he or she is telling me something important. My wife has learned to gently ask me, "Where are you?" which is a sign that I am not present, but rather replaying events from my day.

For you it may be a different physiology and a different manifestation, but the first step in noticing anxiety is to list how it manifests in your body so you can begin intervention early. Anxiety generally starts in either a racing mind, a spinning heart, or a tightening gut. For some, it can be all at once, but as you begin to gain power over anxiety, it will be critical to be able to notice where it begins. Take a moment to consider where, physiologically, your anxiety first shows up. A powerful way to de-escalate anxiety is to diagnose its source: to move from a general "I can't stop thinking about this" or "My heart is racing" to a more specific "The reason I am anxious is because Peter has me in a double bind and a triangle, and it is putting pressure on my people-pleasing idol." Or, "Obsessively thinking about this upcoming difficult meeting will not help preempt the outcome. I believe the lie that worrying will help. Instead I'm going to stop, pray, and ask God to guide me."

Okay, sure, it will take some practice to succinctly diagnose your anxiety, but once you've learned some of the sources and learned to pay attention to your own triggers, you'll be able to diagnose pretty quickly, sometimes even in the moment. Diagnosis de-escalates the power anxiety can have over you because the simple act of naming it reverses the power dynamic. It had you, but by naming it, sometimes out loud or in a prayer, you began to manage it. This is one way we die to self and experience God's resurrection power in our lives.

In my first few weeks of chaplaincy, I brought no self-awareness tools with me, so I didn't realize that after being paged to meet an incoming ambulance, I was praying the same quiet prayer before arriving. The same prayer, every time: *Please, God, don't let it be my wife. Please don't let it be anyone I know.* In those first few weeks I couldn't keep up with all that I was exposed to, and my internal processing was working overtime. Trauma can happen to anyone, and my quiet prayer was an attempt to build a fortress against the very real fear that my wife would be strapped to the gurney with an EMT straddling her, shouting commands, and doing chest compressions. I imagined her with that deep look of terror in her eyes that most trauma patients have when they're wondering if they are going to make it. That prayer is a human prayer, and there is nothing wrong with praying it. But that prayer is a prayer of distance: *Please, God, keep suffering far, far away from my fearful heart.*

And when the person did burst through the double doors, head strapped down, eyes startled, and was in fact neither my wife nor anyone I knew, I prayed a second prayer. *Thank you, God, that it is not my wife or anyone I know.* That prayer, equally human, equally honest, sounds very much like the prayer of the Pharisee in Luke 18:11: "God, I thank you that I am not like other people." And herein lies the problem, for that is a prayer of distance and disconnection. You cannot be present to people when you are creating a protective distance from them. I was physically present but spiritually and emotionally absent. Internal anxiety creates distance between you and the person you are serving because you spend too much energy attending to your anxiety, or, worse yet, you are in its grip but unaware of the squeeze.

Over time, as I became aware of these dual prayers of distance, I continued to pray them but the fear that generated them no longer had the last word. You will read this theme again and again in this book—you may still struggle with anxiety, but it will no longer have the final say. I was able to move through those prayers and see that God was waiting on the other side of my fear and relief, inviting me to trust. I could bring the peace of Christ with me rather than my own fear, and I could attend to the anxiety of the people rather than managing my own. Eventually I could even become aware that the peace of Christ was not something I brought with me, it was already present and at work before I arrived. This is a chronic problem of many leaders: we think God is only with us, not also ahead of us, and so we think we're bringing God into a situation rather than remembering that God is already ahead of us in the situation. This was the fundamental goal of the chaplaincy experience, to be fully present to God and the people God had called me to serve in that moment and to recognize that God is already where I am heading. I think it is the goal of any leader as well.

Following are some sources of internal anxiety that keep you distant and keep you paying too much attention to self. The list isn't exhaustive, and some sources will resonate more than others. My hope is that reading this list will help you generate some sources of your own. By the end of this chapter, you will begin to list your physiological signs and name some sources that trigger you internally. This process can be painful and very personal, and it can take a long time to cultivate, so I ask that you be kind to yourself as you look inside. In no particular order, here are some sources of internal anxiety that block you from trusting God and block you from being fully present to those you lead.

RECOVERING FROM A MISTAKE

If leadership is "knowing what to do" (and most of the time a leader does not know what to do), then leadership is also "making mistakes." All leaders make mistakes, but part of our anxiety is attached to how we respond to making a mistake. How do you react and recover when you make a mistake? I am not talking about the whopper mistakes that place you on the bench for a season; I'm not talking significant moral issues or crimes. I mean mistakes that affect other people, maybe even cause damage; things that you would absolutely do differently next time.

One of my most recent mistakes involved a building program for our church. We had recently moved into a building after years of being portable, setting up and tearing down in public schools. Our church attendance exploded in the new building, and we struggled to keep up with our growth. We needed more space, but were deep in debt because of the building we were in. Should we borrow to build, or pay down debt and crawl our way through?

I led us through a middle-ground solution, raising cash to design a small auxiliary building we could afford that would add some kid space. By the time that building was designed and planned, we had grown more rapidly and it no longer solved enough of our growth issues. The plan also triggered an unforeseen civil engineering expense that escalated the budget. We needed more parking spaces, so we added that to the plan. Slowly it became a much bigger project that simply didn't do enough to relieve our growth issues. After multiple attempts to keep costs in line, our designer failed to meet the budget, so I pulled the plug on the plan. Having previously led a building project, I should have known better, but I was also dealing with a rapidly expanding organization and was stretched in every aspect of my role. Many of us made mistakes along this path, including the designer who kept showing us plans above our budget. But as the organizational leader, I bear responsibility.

My ongoing leadership health is heavily dependent on my capacity to forgive myself for well-meaning mistakes, even mistakes that cost us donated money and a lot of time, mistakes where I have to get up in front of the entire congregation and say, "We thought we were heading down this direction, but we were wrong and we're now going this way." My leadership health is also dependent on my ability to hear criticism of how it should have been done, both by "Monday-morning quarter-backs," who criticize from the sideline, but also from hardworking people in the trenches with me. Mistakes hurt. They bruise the ego. They can also damage good people. But for our organization to thrive, I have to be willing to risk again, open up the possibility of failure again.

Pay attention to how you react after you've made a mistake, and you'll uncover some sources of your anxiety. How long does it take you to recover from a mistake? Do you need to punish yourself when you've made a mistake? Are you reactive when people bring up how it could be done better next time? You can most keenly consider how you deal with a mistake by paying attention to how you communicate it to others. Do you minimize it, justify it, blame, or seek sympathy? The original sin of Adam and Eve in the garden was hiding and blaming. They made a mistake (okay, sure, it was a whopper—the fall of man!). They then proceeded to hide and blame. Is that what you do to cover up a mistake? How do you go about forgiving yourself? How do you seek forgiveness of those you're leading? Making a public mistake hurts because leadership is vulnerable, it is "putting yourself out there," and so when you make a mistake and then don't process it, you'll be tempted to play it safe next time when God is calling you to put yourself back out there.

I tend to be a risk-taker by nature, but some leaders have the opposite problem—they don't make enough mistakes. They are so concerned about doing everything just right, they play it too safe. Their anxiety does not come after the mistake, their anxiety shows up well before they make a leadership decision. They hedge their bets, wait for more data, take polls, anything to avoid committing and potentially doing something wrong. A risk-taking mistake maker learns about anxiety post mortem, but for those of you who are risk averse and cautious, you may need to study your anxiety leading up to a decision. What keeps you from acting? What anxiety are you avoiding by leading this way? How much leadership horsepower are you withholding by playing it so safe? You could explore how "false self" is interfering with God's will in the name of caution. Fear of failure keeps too many leaders from walking by faith.

A lifetime of leadership will involve a lifetime of mistakes. My friend Don Wilson said, "Leaders don't learn from experience, they learn from *evaluated* experience," which means that your ability to grow as a leader is connected to your capacity to examine your mistakes without condemnation and defensiveness. In my leadership context, I am the mistake-maker in chief. I make a lot of them, and I make sure my team does as well. I create a culture that rewards mistakes. We are a high-risk, high-reward church because we walk by faith, and in our best attempts to follow God we are going to get it wrong sometimes. We are going to step out in faith thinking God has called us to a direction when he has not. No one gets it right every time, but we can continue to step out vulnerably after making a public mistake if we're aware of our anxiety.

THE GIANTS ON YOUR SHOULDERS

A common comic strip feature is a person with a devil on one shoulder and an angel on the other, both whispering into her ear, telling her what to do. Rather than some devil and angel, most of us carry our influences and mentors into every leadership encounter. One simple way to lower your anxiety is to pay attention to who is on your shoulders.

I had been a chaplain at the hospital for several weeks when I first discovered the tradition of baptizing stillborn babies. The baptism was mostly a ritual that gave the nurses and parents a meaningful experience for their grief. I came from a tradition that held a very strict theology of baptism—it was only for people old enough to know what they were doing and was only for someone wanting to become a follower of

Christ. Our tradition isn't exactly famous for creative baptism theology, and when I learned about the hospital tradition, I became anxious that I would be asked to baptize a deceased baby and I would have to refuse on principle. I remember one of the chaplains on call coming in the next morning and describing the ceremony overnight, and the huge relief I felt at the close call. Labor and Delivery was my unit, and I was fortunate to not be on call that night, but it was only a matter of time. Was my anxiety theologically driven? Partially, yes, but mostly it was driven by Bible college professors, each sitting on my shoulders watching over my theology, judging me. What would they think of this situation? Would I stand up for "the truth" or would I acquiesce?

During one of my overnight marathons, the pager woke me at 2:00 a.m. and summoned me to Labor and Delivery. I walked up to the desk and the nurse told me that a young couple had had a stillborn baby and wanted it to be baptized. I walked into the room with giants on my shoulders telling me not to do it, that by doing it I would be violating the very core of my belief. I was unable to connect with the grieving couple in any meaningful way because of the energy it took attending to the giants.

The giants on my shoulders are real people, I can name them today, but what made them giants is my imagination. The way I imagined them talking to me was harsh and dogmatic, and they expressed profound disappointment in me. In reality those fine mentors may have been much more gracious and understanding than my imagination allowed, but that is what happens with the giants on our shoulders—they are no longer fully human, we make them two-dimensional and they gain power over us. As I walked into the room, I was so afraid of what my mentors would think that I didn't have enough energy to focus on the mentors and this young couple. And yes, if you're wondering, I held that tiny, premature, stillborn baby in the palm of my hand and baptized him. It took months to admit to anyone beyond my wife.

Knowing and naming the giants on your shoulders can relieve you of feeding and giving energy to them. Sometimes the giants on your shoulders are literally living with you at home. I know a leader whose giant is a spouse. He comes home and vents about someone and his spouse sends various forms of the same message: "Don't let them get away with that!" And so when he is in a leadership environment, he is not only attending to the conflict, he is also attending to the disappointment of his wife when he concedes or compromises. That is way too much pressure. Let the mentors shrivel away so you can attend to the real people in front of you rather than the imagined tyrants on your shoulders. And if the imagined tyrants are actual tyrants, you can deal with them in their own time, but no need to add to your load by dealing with them when they aren't even in the room.

BLIND SPOT KNOWLEDGE
AND FEELING EXPOSED

The worst kind of knowledge is knowledge someone else has about you that you don't have about yourself, but as soon as they share it you know it is true. Blind spot knowledge. You suddenly feel exposed and at risk, yet at the same time, you know there is truth there and you're thrust into two choices: be open to this knowledge and move toward it or deny it. The most common denial technique is to decide there is something wrong with the person who named it. Nobody likes to be given blind spot knowledge, but without it, we don't grow.

Peter is a local lead pastor who shared about blind spot knowledge.

Our staff recently attended an annual leadership summit. For two days we experienced a fire hose of powerful information and inspiring ideas. Knowing these experiences can often cause strong excitement but little actual change in an organization, I had our staff write out specifically what their highlights and takeaways were. We met a week later to all share how we were going to do things differently because of what we learned through this summit. I figured this would be really helpful for the staff. You know, they really need this kind of stuff. I am such a helpful leader for putting this together for them.

The meeting went great. Many shared how they were going to tweak this and change that. As I listened I realized many referenced one of the speakers who talked about "how-ing" ideas instead of "wow-ing" ideas. The speaker's point was that many leaders squash the dreams of those under them by always asking how some new idea is going to be done, instead of simply saying "Wow" and encouraging the staff member to work on figuring it out. As I heard multiple people on my staff reference this idea, I decided to step out on a limb. I asked the entire staff if they experienced me as a "wow" leader or a "how" leader. I wish I would have answered first, because I know I am a "wow" leader. I can give you examples! Trust me, I am! Except that is not what the staff said. Well, a few of them did, but the majority of the staff looked me in the eye and said they experience me "how-ing" them to death. It was a difficult moment for me. It was a vulnerable moment for me. It was a very important moment for me. My perception of my leadership was not correct and I needed my staff to help me see how my issues of control were affecting their ability to dream.

Blind spot knowledge. By definition, you'll never see it on your own. How do you respond when someone else sees it? Among my leaders, we tend to know one another's and help one another with it. I will never eliminate my blind spot, but I want to know how it negatively impacts my people so we can mitigate it together. It is never an easy conversation!

JUDGMENT

Judgment limits the scope of our leadership because it shrinks the array of people we can lead. Judgment creates distance and also makes assumptions about a person that may not be true. We all hold a variety of judgments, even people who celebrate how nonjudgmental they are. By naming the types of people we judge, we can move past that initial obstacle and lead a much broader range of people. Naming our judgment keeps us from dehumanizing real people in our head and helps us to be able to serve them. I encourage you to write an actual list of the types of people you judge. Don't name the people! Just list the characteristics of people you judge. You'd be surprised at how long that list is, how many people it encompasses, and how it limits your ability to lead them. You may also be surprised at how petty some of your judgments are.

I was raised to always wear a seat belt; in my family not wearing a seat belt is two steps lower than first-degree murder. Wearing a seat belt is simply what responsible people do. At one point in my chaplaincy, I was paged to the ER to find a distraught woman in the family lounge waiting to hear an update on several children behind the double doors. She was on carpool duty for her son and his friends, and she hadn't buckled any of them. When she ran the red light and caused an accident, all the children were ejected from the van. She was the only one buckled, and the ER team was fighting to keep the kids alive.

She was suffering, but I was angry at her. Why? Because she violated my standards of behavior and also because her tragedy was so preventable. I judge people who don't use a seat belt and people who make easily avoidable mistakes. I was far along enough in my awareness to name my judgment in a prayer and repent of it, but what really freed me was the evening news. This mum was on the news; her accident became a feature that night. The news anchor gave a quick overview of the accident and then handed off to the local reporter who was at the scene. The minivan was a twisted wreck with its windshield missing. The reporter made sure to point out that the kids were not wearing seat belts and then proceeded to show where they were ejected through the window. She closed with a report that the kids were in critical condition at the hospital. I was sitting right next to the mother as she watched the news report. The mother was watching everyone in the ER waiting room. They were watching the news and then looking at her. But then it got worse.

The evening news did a spin-off story on seat belt safety and why seat belts are the simplest, safest way for kids to travel. I understand why they did this, and I suppose if that story prevented another adult from making the same awful mistake, then it was worth it. But I will never forget the overwhelming shame this woman exhibited. She was completely exposed to the entire ER waiting room and to me. My heart broke for her because rather than stay behind the safe distance of judgment, I was in close proximity. I was sitting right next to her and I felt the judgment people were sending her way, the same judgment I had to repent of moments earlier. And what is really weird is I felt judged by association just because I was sitting next to her, as if I was somehow silently endorsing her behavior. I have been haunted by the experience ever since. The simple fact is, I am significantly more judgmental of people than God is. Knowing and naming your judgments is a simple tool to help de-escalate your anxiety.

VALUES VIOLATIONS

Related to judgment, anxiety can be triggered when someone violates an unspoken value of ours. Sometimes we don't even know what we value until someone violates it and we find ourselves unreasonably angry in response. Our punishment does not fit the crime. One of my biggest triggers is respect, and I had to work on this when my kids were very young. When their friends came over to play, some of their friends were barely showing respect toward adults. I found myself unnecessarily angry at the kids because they had violated my values. I have a friend who is triggered by lack of courtesy. He will happily drop what he is doing to help someone when asked, but if someone presumes on him or is discourteous, his response is anger. Why? Because he so deeply values courteousness—he extends it to others and expects it in return. What are your deep values that get triggered when someone violates them? It isn't about compromising your values, it is about getting past your response to be able to connect with those people.

Sometimes we're triggered not by a violation of values, but by someone who exhibits the same shadow we have. I get easily triggered by arrogant, self-righteous people. It is too much like looking in the mirror. *Ouch*. I can connect with those people by recognizing in them what I despise in myself and moving past it.

ISOLATIONISM AND EXCEPTIONALISM

There is no way around the inherent loneliness of leadership, but some of our anxiety is caused by isolationism—not the very real occasion when a leader stands alone, but the internal need of a leader to feel alone in order to gain something for self. Some leaders feel alone not by self-pity, but by self-aggrandizement. Such a person believes that other people are mere mortals, but he is unique, exceptional. Whether your tendency is toward isolationism ("No one understands") or exceptionalism ("No one can do it like me"), the danger is the same: the need to feel like you are "the only one." There is something deeply satisfying in believing the old song, "Nobody knows the trouble I've seen, nobody knows but Jesus." It is some version of "God and me are the only ones who get it," except it is very rarely true.

While every leader does face a true moment of standing alone, most of the time we have more company than we care to admit. We don't want to admit it because we find comfort in self-pity. Isolationism is a deadly form of anxiety mostly because it is very rarely true, but we self-isolate to prop up the myth.

The need to feel exceptional is the flip side of feeling alone, its source isn't self-pity, but self-aggrandizement. Exceptionalism feeds the false beliefs that "I alone can fix this" or "No one can do it as well as me." Rather than thanking God for the team God has given you, you're looking over your people's shoulders for the perfect team member who doesn't exist. News flash: you're not so perfect yourself, but you live by the double standard of giving yourself grace for your own imperfections and believing everyone else should be like you or better. Exceptionalism is one of the deadliest ways to kill a team culture and is an entrenched form of self-righteousness.

ANGER FANTASIES AND THE NEED FOR AN ENEMY

You're driving down the road picturing a conversation or a fight with another person, usually someone who has emailed you or made a painful comment in a meeting, or someone who has a history of causing you pain. As you play it out in your mind, you're not only defending yourself, you are unloading on that person, and at the end of this anger fantasy the person apologizes, sees the error of her ways, and declares that you are indeed justified and she is in the wrong.

Yeah, I've never had that happen either.

Anger fantasies are insidious because they feel so good and are the natural way for your brain to make sense of your emotions. But they are dangerous because you are dehumanizing the person in your mind. You mentally strip her of her dimension and nuance in order to be the better person. This is self-righteousness at its deadliest, because you can indulge it without ever having to really engage the person.

DOUBT (SELF-DOUBT AND DOUBT IN GOD)

Doubt is a giant topic that could use its own book-length treatment. It is the ever-present companion to most leaders and it comes in a couple of forms: doubt in your own ability and doubt in God.

Doubt in Your Own Ability

This is also known as the imposter syndrome. It is the plaguing feeling that you don't belong in this leadership role. You are ill-equipped, don't know what you're doing, and, worse yet, one day someone is going to expose you for the fraud that you are. Some people live double lives, hiding a significant moral issue, but for most leaders the imposter syndrome is the inner voice that says, *You are not enough; one day someone better will show up and everyone will wonder why you were here so long.*

I spent the first decade as a lead pastor battling imposter syndrome. For those keeping track, I've been a lead pastor for thirteen years, so the vast majority of them were spent wondering when the real pastor was going to show up and lead more competently than I was leading. Imposter syndrome whispers, "If people knew how little you know what you are doing, they would conclude that you don't belong." For me, this really came to light in my early preaching. When I became a lead pastor, I had more than a decade of fruitful ministry experience, but never in the lead chair. I had preached many times before, but never every week. Wow, was that ever a game changer. I was learning to preach in front of the people I was guiding, week after week. I have since concluded that a preacher needs 70 to 120 concurrent sermons to really find her or his voice. That means for my first couple of years I was still settling into my point of view, my unique way of preaching, and it was pretty painful for all of us, preacher and listeners both. Imposter syndrome was whispering that a real preacher should do this. It is humbling for a leader to learn in front of the people he or she is leading.

Doubt in God

My year as a chaplain plunged me into a season of doubt that plagued me for many years. I was twenty-four when I began chaplaincy, and I had been a Christian for about a decade. I had spent my late teens working in the business world before going to Bible college. I thought my faith was grounded, but the onslaught of death and pain and people asking why multiple times per day shook what I knew to be true about God and life.

After chaplaincy I attended an academically rigorous seminary, and the professors exposed us to a range of perspectives on Jesus and Scripture. I remember reading brilliant scholars who would show that heaven is an invented human construct and that Jesus' miracles were not real, they were simply retrofitted to him by his followers to make sense of his death. Jesus' life on earth ended in death, not resurrection as I had always believed.

The combination of pain and trauma one year and then academic skepticism the next really did a number on my faith. At the time my religious tradition did not have much room for doubt; therefore I had to hunt for mentors to guide me through my confusion. I have thanked God over and over again for people like Philip Yancey, Frederick Buechner, and Walter Brueggemann, who openly write and speak about doubt as a normative Christian experience. Of course, the early church fathers and mothers wrote extensively about the dark night of the soul, but I was not exposed to them until seminary. At the time I thought I was losing my faith, not ideal for a pastoral vocation, but these authors helped me to see that I was not losing my faith, it was simply being reformed and reframed. "Orientation, disorientation, reorientation" is how Brueggemann described it. But so often the disorientation comes suddenly and the reorientation takes longer than we want, especially when we're reorienting to a place we've never been. Reorientation takes longer if we're trying to reorient back to where we were. Doubt in God is especially difficult for a teaching leader. If you are a preacher or if your role is to shape the theology and belief of your people, how do you handle your own doubt?

Those early, intense years of plaguing doubt are gone, but I still battle doubt on a regular basis. The years 2007 to 2012 were some of the most intense and painful seasons of my life. Our church was paying an interest-only mortgage for land on which we could not afford to build. At the same time, we suffered the tragic loss of many of our fine young leaders to death: car accident, cancer, ALS. These leaders were all my close friends who left young families behind. It was a deeply painful time to lead our church in a funeral on Saturday and then get up to preach a sermon on hope on Sunday.

The church was also at high risk of losing our land. The economy had plunged into recession, and the bank refused to refinance our loan, instead planning to auction it off and come after the signatories for the difference. My name was on the loan and my family could have lost our house. To make this story brief, our land was unmarketable because the city had added a very strict zoning onto it after we purchased it to severely limit development, but somewhat miraculously we were able to attract a buyer who would buy half our land for a good price and enter a shared development agreement that would decrease our own construction costs. It appeared as if God had miraculously opened a door for us. After months of planning and moving ahead, the city quietly gave the developer a different property on which to build, and, as a result we lost the deal. We were back in the clutches of the bank for repossession.

Sometimes you think you see the hand of God, and then you follow what you believe is God's leading and run smack into a brick wall. What then? Sometimes you get up to preach but are unsure of what is really true. What then? Sometimes your own faith is on a slow reorientation and you need time and space to figure it out. What then?

By the time I became a lead pastor, I was in my early thirties and a decade into my relationship with doubt. I knew the only way to live with integrity was to share my own doubt with our congregation. Even today people know my doubt; they know when I thought I was leading us to God's will but wasn't; they know when I experience the very human cry of "Lord I believe, help my unbelief." Of course one of the reasons they know it is many of them struggle with it as well. And by their pastor sharing doubt, it gave them permission to bring their own doubt into the light. Doubt is a constant companion, but like many of these other triggers, getting it out in the open where there is oxygen and blue sky keeps it from debilitating me.

But doubt without an outlet can generate massive anxiety. When a leader's private life is significantly incongruent with her public life, the leader is in grave danger. If you struggle with imposter syndrome because you are hiding a destructive habit, or if you find your own faith slipping into an unknown future, I highly encourage you to find safe people to whom you can talk. Leaders don't naturally see the people they are leading as the safe people they can share with, but if your culture is healthy, sharing with your people may be the best move. Tragically for too many leaders, the people they are leading are the least safe people to share this with, and that only adds to anxiety's grip. Who can you talk to? Take a moment to write some names down and take the risk of sharing your doubt.

Obviously, this is a fast pass at some sources of internal anxiety. Naming and knowing the sources is a vital step in reducing anxiety's impact on your life. I have written about some of the sources I most struggle with and that I see in others, but this list may have spurred you to recognize some other sources in yourself. Power over anxiety begins when you succinctly identify the sources in concrete ways; it then continues when you tell some friends you trust.

Finally, a few words on personality profiles: StrengthsFinder, DiSC, Myers-Briggs, Enneagram. They're all helpful tools in clarifying a leader's unique contribution and wiring. My concern is not what these profiles teach us, it is how we are tempted to use them to limit what we do. The profile is not the problem; the way we can hide behind them might be. I know a discipleship pastor who discovered through some of these personality assessments that she is an introvert who needs time alone to reenergize. It's important to know what you need, but she discovered that she was using her profile as an excuse to not engage people. She had told herself, "Because I am a high introvert, I cannot expend energy talking to these people," but we often have more capacity than our profiles might suggest. More importantly, faithfulness to God will involve doing things that are way outside your wiring and personality. The martyrs and missionaries of the last few hundred years did not have these modern tools to say, "I'd love to do that, but it doesn't fit my wiring." I'm grateful Paul didn't take these profile assessments or he may have written, "I can do some things within my wiring and energy zone through [Christ] who gives me strength" (Phil. 4:13, paraphrased).

There is wisdom in paying attention to wiring, personality, and personality traits when choosing a vocation. Making sure you are in a sweet spot is a key ingredient for long-term leadership health. However, every leader I respect has a dual attitude of, "Whatever it takes" and "I can do all things through Christ who gives me strength." Sometimes you simply have to do what you'd prefer not to do or are not wired to do. We are more resilient, flexible, and able than we realize. And on the other side of our personality profile is God, inviting us to depend on God's strength and leading. Our God-given capacity might be beyond what we think, and the task at hand might require us to move well outside our wiring. Sometimes you simply have to do something you're not wired to do for the sake of the cause, or push beyond your natural tendency in order to be faithful to what God is calling you to do.

So, what sources of anxiety resonate with you? Or did this list trigger others you want to discuss? Knowing and naming your sources does not eliminate anxiety: it reduces the plaguing power anxiety has on your life. For those whose anxiety sources are connected to trauma or abuse, I encourage you to process with a trusted professional who knows how to guide you. Awareness is one thing, being able to pay attention and die to it is another altogether, and that is a skill that will take time. Twenty years after beginning this journey, I mostly have the same triggers, but the difference is they no longer bind me as often as they used to. This can be true of you as well.

DISCUSSION QUESTIONS

1. How does anxiety show up physiologically in you (examples: spinning mind, racing heart, tightening gut)? Once you identify that physiology, try to list a few signs that anxiety is in play.
2. Which of the sources above do you most struggle with? What does that look like in your life?
3. Are you able to name any sources of internal anxiety that are not listed in this chapter?
4. What kinds of people do you judge? What values do you find being violated? How might naming those improve your capacity to serve those very people?
5. Can you share an example of how your anxiety has blocked your ability to be present with someone? How about how it has blocked your capacity to notice God?

four

IDOLS, VOWS, AND
THE STORIES WE
TELL OURSELVES

It ain't what you don't know that gets you into trouble.
It's what you know for sure that just ain't so.

—AUTHOR UNKNOWN

Having listed various sources of internal anxiety, now we go deeper by focusing on two significant sources: idols and childhood vows. What we live for when we're not living for Jesus (idols) and what we believe to be true that is not always true (childhood vows) combine to form the stories we tell ourselves and can significantly derail leadership. When we are under pressure, exhausted, or feeling threatened, we revert to depending on the stories we tell ourselves rather than the story of God. I think one of the reasons God's story is called the good news is because it is in direct competition with the stories we tell ourselves, which are so often bad news (or perhaps more precisely, they are good news for now, bad news long term). The reason to do the difficult and very personal work of dethroning idols and repenting of childhood vows is to experience the freedom that Jesus offers his followers. We depend on idols and vows as a false security to get us through pain and to keep a false self intact. Jesus said, "The truth will set you free" (John 8:32) and Paul said, "It is for freedom that Christ has set us free" (Gal. 5:1), so we do this difficult and personal work for a deeper experience of freedom.

We all have secrets, idols, compulsions, drivers, and so forth that can limit our leadership and our families' and organizations' health. In this chapter we expose these as part of our self-awareness journey, but we also expose them for the sake of the people we lead, so our own issues that stunt us do not also stunt our organizations or families. Some leaders leave their organizations because they have entrenched their own problems into the organizations. So rather than stay and grow, they leave, only to bring their issues to the next organizations. Instead of that, we bring our issues into the light and ask God to sift them and ultimately to get them out of the way of our following Jesus. We also bring them into awareness to discover that God has been using our life experiences, including our painful experiences, to forge us into the followers he wants us to be.

The story you tell yourself is a subconscious, ever-present filter between the outside world and your brain making meaning of everything. The great challenge of it is that until you examine it, you don't even know it is there. But even now, if you pay careful attention, you will notice a filter in your head. As you are reading this, you may notice a filter telling you what you think about what you're reading.

The voice is saying, "That's exactly right!" or "Wow, this author is overly sensitive" or "I still can't believe he thinks we shouldn't be like Jesus!" It acts as a mediator and interpreter between you and the world and its power is strengthened by your unawareness of it.

The story you tell yourself is often forged in pain and suspicion and can significantly limit your leadership scope. One way to notice it is when you take a singular truth and make it universally true. Something painful happened in your past and you then project that onto every future scenario that is similar. Another way to notice the story is to pay attention to "same species syndrome." A couple of church pastors in your past used power to cause you pain. This is a singular truth, but your internal filter makes it universally true: now all pastors are suspect. This universal truth is reinforced by *same species syndrome*. The previous pain came at the hand of some church leaders; therefore all church leaders are highly suspicious.

You look for evidence that all pastors are suspect, and let's face it, any organizational leader with power who can invoke God is going to be at high risk of misusing power. Still, you approach the next pastor with high suspicion, waiting for him or her to let you down by a misuse of power. You read misuse of power into the leader's actions and you assume the worst even when there is no objective evidence to back you up. Same species syndrome. Deadly, but very common in the stories we tell ourselves. The story can be reinforced into a self-fulfilling prophecy if you are not careful. Sometimes we project so strongly that we actually create the very reality we are trying to avoid. Leaders who are gifted communicators can be especially at risk for infecting reality with the stories they tell themselves.

This is one way our false self most obviously shows up. It interprets everything outside of our brain and places meaning on it and then infects everything we say and do. The story we tell ourselves infects reality and shapes what actually "is" and turns it into what we think "is." God is on the other side of what we think "is," which is why we access so much power and freedom if we can move beyond the stories we tell ourselves.

The other problem with this filter is that it fills in the gap of ignorance. When you think about it, there exists a massive gap between what we know and what we think we know. I once worked at a church with a staff member who was highly introverted and introspective, so as he was walking down the hall of the church building, if someone would say "Hello," he would not say hello back. That is objective reality, but things get sketchy fast when we attach meaning to reality and create a new reality. People would pass by and after he didn't acknowledge them, they would make meaning of it.

The story we tell ourselves infects reality and shapes what actually "is" and turns it into what we think "is."

"The reason he didn't say hello is because he is offended by me." Or, "He disapproves of me and doesn't like me."

Oh, the problems this simple issue generated among staff and volunteers. To be sure, this staff member could have used some lessons in social etiquette, and I am not defending his behavior, but the emotion and heat that his lack of greeting generated was stunning. In reality, he may have been thinking about how bad last night's leftovers were, but in the mind of the people walking by, his lack of greeting was an intentional dismissal of their existence. If we are prone to insecurity or needing people to like us, this can quickly become a nightmare, because we feel compelled to act on the meaning we're making. So the next time we see him, we might awkwardly avoid him, or we might make an extra effort to engage him, but either way, we're solving a problem that may not actually exist, and our well-meaning attempt now creates a real problem. The leftovers guy is now having to manage people glaring at him, or someone trying to hug him, or any number of unnatural responses.

Jeanie Duck said that in the absence of information, "people will connect the dots in the most pathological way possible."[1] Often the stories we tell ourselves are full of all manner of pathology and half-truths. The good news of Jesus is the story no longer gets the final word. You can't really shut off the story you tell yourself, but you can tell it to go away once in a while. This inner voice is often suspicious of what your hear, but who is suspicious of it? What if you doubt your doubt to dislodge its power? You can begin to pay attention to the gap between objective facts, "He didn't say hello back," and the meaning you make of it, "Clearly he doesn't like me." On the other side of your assumption you'll find a much wilder and exhilarating reality than you can possibly imagine: the story of God. The Truth. The "good news." These stories, and we all have hundreds of them, are forged and reinforced by two particular sources of anxiety: idols and childhood vows.

IDOLS

"Since, then, you have been raised with Christ, set your hearts on things above, where Christ is, seated at the right hand of God. Set your minds on things above, not on earthly things. For you died, and your life is now hidden with Christ in God. When Christ, who is your life, appears, then you also will appear with him in glory. Put to death, therefore, whatever belongs to your earthly nature: sexual immorality, impurity, lust, evil desires and greed, which is idolatry." (Col. 3:1–5)

One of the most consistent, recurring topics of the entire Bible is idolatry. At first glance we dismiss idolatry as something quaint that people used to do, but now that we put a man on the moon and invented free Wi-Fi, we have outgrown such quaint behavior. But recently many Christian thinkers have helped us see the prevalence of idolatry. Tim Keller preached and wrote extensively about idols. In his presentation,

"Preaching the Gospel," he defined an idol as: "Any good thing that you make into an ultimate thing."[2] Money, for example, is a good thing, but those who make it an ultimate thing are idolatrous. A person's opinion may be a good thing, but make it an ultimate thing and you end up exhausted, trying to keep that idol happy. An idol is anything other than Jesus that you must have to be okay. In the Bible an idol was almost always a tangible object and often forged by someone. Today, an idol is more commonly a heart desire, an impulse, or a compulsion that we think we need to have in order to be okay.

Tim Keller described more about idols:

> An idol is a "functional savior." Why do we lie, or fail to love, or break our promises, or live selfishly? Of course, the general answer is "Because we are weak and sinful," but the specific answer is that there is something besides Jesus Christ that we feel we must have to be happy, something that is more important to our heart than God, something that is enslaving our heart through inordinate desires. The key to change and even to self-understanding is therefore to identify the idols of the heart.[3]

Idols are not immediately easy to identify in your life, but one sure way to begin is to pay attention to when you are anxious, feeling threatened, or needing something in order to be settled.

One way you know something is an idol is that you sacrifice time and power to get it. You can also spend some time looking at what you daydream about, what your nightmare scenario is, and what you repeatedly worry about. The common thread of an idol is "I need it to be okay," so when you find yourself anxious or deeply unsettled, it may be because you are not getting what you think you need to be okay.

My locker holds a hefty collection of idols, and when left unchecked, I feed and water them on a regular basis. Here are a few of mine: the need to be understood, the need to be right, the need to be liked by people, the need to be impressive. I first identified these idols about fifteen years ago and have been battling their power and influence in my life ever since. They never really go away, but I have learned to mitigate their impact through applying the gospel to my life.

You can imagine how preaching puts tremendous pressure on these particular idols. Public speaking is an exercise in miscommunication, and my style of preaching includes spontaneous comments and unscripted stories once in a while. This can bind me into wanting people's approval but also being misunderstood and having people disagree with me. I have grown more by battling my idols

An idol is anything other than Jesus that you must have to be okay.

that are raw and exposed in the pulpit than almost any other spiritual endeavor. Every time I step up to preach, I have a choice—am I going to feed my collection of idols or am I going to die to that need and speak for God?

Jaymie served as an elder in a church plant for its first several years. One of her idols is needing to be recognized for her ability and performance. She said,

I became an early leader in a church plant and took on defending the mission and vision of the church at all costs. But when the church hit some bumps and seemed to be changing directions, I couldn't separate my following of Jesus from my serving of this church. I couldn't find my contributing place amid the changes. It's not enough for me to belong because I am invited into God's kingdom; I have to belong by performing. So when I stepped away from serving and contributing, I was totally lost. It cut to the core of my identity. My response was one of anger, "Okay fine, Jesus, build your church without me." Building the church had become an idol on the road to following Jesus, and serving the church was a sophisticated way of tapping my childhood need for love and approval by performing well. The humbling thing with an idol is it is always in my life, ready to take hold. Now I measure the grip of an idol by my emotional reaction. My emotional reaction is a fear that I have failed, haven't performed well to people's expectations. My need to control a situation can mean I talk too much and over-direct a group. When people confront me about this, I move into a way of thinking of, "I have to fix what is wrong with me. I must make it right." I struggle to allow God to work in the mess of this. I need to track down each fire and fix it on my own, but after all that effort, I am still left with discord and contempt. I get into an obsession of how to perfect the mess even when I know it's not my place to perfect it. My idol enslaves my thoughts and that's where I know God is doing work in me. If I can step off the emotional reaction and see my idol at play, the situation that causes all that initial anxiety becomes a gift to me.

Isaiah spoke at length on the power of idols. His ancient words continue to convict us of the power of idolatry in our lives.

> The blacksmith takes a tool
>> and works with it in the coals;
> he shapes an idol with hammers,
>> he forges it with the might of his arm.
> He gets hungry and loses his strength;
>> he drinks no water and grows faint.
> The carpenter measures with a line
>> and makes an outline with a marker;
> he roughs it out with chisels
>> and marks it with compasses.
> He shapes it in human form,
>> human form in all its glory,
>> that it may dwell in a shrine.

He cut down cedars,
>> or perhaps took a cypress or oak.
He let it grow among the trees of the forest,
>> or planted a pine, and the rain made it grow.
It is used as fuel for burning;
>> some of it he takes and warms himself,
>> he kindles a fire and bakes bread.
But he also fashions a god and worships it;
>> he makes an idol and bows down to it.
Half of the wood he burns in the fire;
>> over it he prepares his meal,
>> he roasts his meat and eats his fill.
He also warms himself and says,
>> "Ah! I am warm; I see the fire."
From the rest he makes a god, his idol;
>> he bows down to it and worships.
He prays to it and says,
>> "Save me! You are my god!"
They know nothing, they understand nothing;
>> their eyes are plastered over so they cannot see,
>> and their minds closed so they cannot understand.
No one stops to think,
>> no one has the knowledge or understanding to say,
"Half of it I used for fuel;
>> I even baked bread over its coals,
>> I roasted meat and I ate.
Shall I make a detestable thing from what is left?
>> Shall I bow down to a block of wood?"
Such a person feeds on ashes; a deluded heart misleads him;
>> he cannot save himself, or say,
>> "Is not this thing in my right hand a lie?"

(ISA. 44:12–20)

Isaiah was having fun showcasing these skilled craftsmen who took some wood that was only available because God provided rain for the tree to grow. The carpenter then used some wood to make an idol, some to burn a fire for food, and he then proceeded to thank the idol made from the wood for the food! I wish I could laugh at the carpenter along with Isaiah, but this hits too close to home. God gave me gifts to use for God's glory, but I turn them into idols and quickly forget the source, choosing instead to seek comfort and security from the gifts rather than the God who gave them.

CHILDHOOD VOWS

As a child I was always the ball bearings for my whole family;
I thought I was indispensable to their survival, preventing
hard metal from grinding against hard metal, so the family
didn't come to a broken, screeching, metallic halt.
—ANNE LAMOTT

A childhood vow is a promise you make to yourself as a child, either consciously or subconsciously, that informs the way you see and operate in the world. A childhood vow is often forged out of pain and neglect, but can sometimes be made in the chase of pleasure. The challenge of a childhood vow is that it becomes deeply entrenched into our false selves and keeps us bound to bad news instead of the good news of Jesus. Jim Herrington has taught and written extensively on the power of childhood vows. He says,

Vows put our past into our future, thereby keeping us in bondage to them. When we experience pain in our early years, trust was ruptured and forgiveness withheld. Out of that pain we each made some vows about how we were going to be, how we were going to "do relationships" as adults. These vows became obstacles. These obstacles became strongholds. Uncovering our wounds and our unmet needs and allowing God to bring healing to those places in our experience accelerates our growth.[4]

Jim created the following diagram to help map out this process. The vow is created from the top down, the story you tell yourself becomes the way you see the world from the bottom up.

You have experience (s)

You make meaning of the experience (s)

You make a vow based on the meaning (s)

Your false self is created

**Habits of disobedience become
embedded and feed the false self**

The arrow on the left side of the page shows the progression of the process. The arrow on the right side demonstrates how the habitual dependence on the vow reinforces the false self. The false self is anchored in the vow rather than in the good news of Jesus. Living into the vow reinforces the meaning that you make of your experience and adds power to the story you tell yourself. Naming and repenting of a vow can free you of anxiety and open you to healing and freedom that God offers. This, once again, is why God's story is good news and the stories we tell ourselves are so often bad news. Vows lock and narrow our future, they bind us to same species syndrome, they keep us flailing and stuck in recurring patterns. Childhood vows are like childhood clothes. We needed them as kids and they fit well, but as we grew into adulthood, they became constricting and began to strangle us. A vow suffocates your future and increases your anxiety, because you are living out of that vow rather than by faith in God.

One of the signs of a vow is using a superlative like *never* or *always*. "I will *never* raise my kid the way my mother raised me" or "I will *never* open my heart to someone and get crushed again."

Another way to uncover a vow is to notice when you use *should*, *ought*, or *must*. "I must protect my mother from my abusive father by distracting him when he drinks." Or "I should always do it perfectly because imperfection receives condemnation." Several years ago, I was sitting with my friend Greg, and he expressed that he was fed up with his self-talk. He said, "I constantly 'should' all over myself. I am my own worst critic. I should do this, I must do that. It's all too much." That woke me up! But he offered a needed stark statement to show how contaminating shoulding and oughting is. Stop shoulding all over yourself!

Of course, vows can be positive as well—not just moving away from pain, but moving toward pleasure. But just because they are positive doesn't mean they are any less dangerous and constricting. I remember the first time I gave a significant speech in public and the crowd was really engaged during the speech, lots of laughter and reaction, and then after the speech I received all sorts of affirmation from folks. It felt really good, and in that moment I made a vow to get that feeling again. Years later I became a professional public speaker. Of course, I track my vocation to a call from God, but also partly from a vow I made to seek pleasure and affirmation. You can imagine the damage I can do to my own soul and to good people when I am operating out of that vow rather than out of obedience to God.

Vows can also be genuinely necessary to get us through childhood. I have a friend whose father was an alcoholic and became highly violent when drunk. My friend made a childhood vow that skillfully allowed him to protect himself, his brother, and his mother from his father's violence. His vow literally helped him to survive childhood, but of course it strangled his adulthood, forcing all manner of legalism of always having to be right and moral. His vow told him he must protect everyone all the time. God's power and God's people are forgotten when this vow is telling him to step in and save the day again and again.

While Scripture speaks frequently about idols, it does not directly address childhood vows. But it does remind us of the deep and mysterious power of words: words spoken and words believed. I used to be puzzled by the story of Isaac, Jacob, and Esau (Gen. 27). Jacob tricked his dad into giving the family blessing to him instead of his brother, but there was no signed contract, it was all words. Why couldn't Isaac retract his promise when he discovered he'd been swindled by Jacob?

Today we toss words around flippantly. We live in an overabundance of words, but Isaac knew the way words actually work. When Esau found out about the deception, he begged his dad, "Bless me too, my father!" (v. 38). But Isaac accurately stated that he had no more blessing to give. He had already given it away. I think that is because Isaac knew that words not only have emotional power, but also spiritual power, and this is why a childhood vow has so much power over us. Those words lodge deep in our soul between the pain we experienced and the absence of what we needed in those moments. We needed protection, unconditional love, warmth, but we got pain instead and we made a vow to protect from pain.

This is why I think the gospel of Jesus is such incredibly good news, because what you may not have gotten as a child, Jesus freely offers without condition: identity, acceptance, love. The reason a vow is so insidious and dangerous is because it often affects us without our conscious awareness. We are secretly telling ourselves how reality is going to be rather than what really is. Jesus warned us to take care in making a vow when he said: "But I tell you, do not swear an oath at all: either by heaven, for it is God's throne; or by the earth, for it is his footstool; or by Jerusalem, for it is the city of the Great King. And do not swear by your head, for you cannot make even one hair white or black. All you need to say is simply 'Yes' or 'No'; anything beyond this comes from the evil one" (Matt. 5:34–37).

Ellen is an old friend of mine who recently shared one of her childhood vows.

> I basically grew up as an only child—my siblings had already moved out of the house. My dad is a strong man who values his privacy and wants things to be done the right way (his way). My mom is like a combination of a hypochondriac, hoarder, and "the world's out to get me" type of person. This was not always the best for their marriage. What I remember of my childhood includes all of the times I heard my mom and my dad get in fights—my mom would say something out of the blue that she believed was her truth, and my dad would get annoyed and would call her crazy. She would get offended that her own husband didn't believe her and the teeth would come out. The yelling would increase until I couldn't take it anymore, and I usually found myself in the middle of the two, begging them to stop.
>
> Through my teen years my mother's mental health deteriorated. She cut off extended family, grew paranoid, blamed people for things they had never done, and made everyone walk on eggshells around her. My dad's side of the family asked her to stop coming to family functions—Christmas, Thanksgiving, reunions, visits—the whole thing. Then my mom's side of the family started doing the same thing until she stopped talking to all of them. My dad always picked their side over my mom, and I had enough of it. I decided that since nobody wanted my mom, I would protect her, stand up for her, care for her. That's how I got through my childhood.

After learning about childhood vows, I started seeing these

same instincts of protection and "mothering" show up in my daily life. I constantly wanted to do whatever I could for people to make them feel loved and respected, but I would always go overboard. I would see a perfectly capable person in need of one thing and I would take it upon myself to fix their entire life, it seemed. I run after those who are misunderstood and stand up for them even when they can do it themselves. When I visited my parents on vacation, I reverted back to the way I survived as a child even though I am a fully-grown adult now. I would nearly smother my mother with protection and care even when she never asked for it.

Recently I have had to repent from my childhood vow. My duty to save my mom was turning into an unnecessary habit that made other people feel less powerful than they were and that exhausted and frustrated me. I was able to relax into the truth that I need a Savior more and more, and that this same Savior can help others with or without me. I am still a helpful person, I still have a deep passion to stand up for those who need a voice, but it is less driven by my vow and more by how God has forged my childhood experiences for his glory. And the best part? After I moved out of my house and after I refused to step into my parents' arguments, my parents' relationship changed dramatically. They have learned how to deal with each other and they have actually started to like each other again. After I repented of my need to be the savior, a deeper experience of God's grace came into my life.

Vows don't go away on their own; we don't outgrow them. Instead, they keep us stunted and we have to shed them to be free. Identifying and repenting of a childhood vow is a personal experience and is best done with someone you trust: a friend or a therapist. Part of the repentance process is to write a letter of repentance from your vow and to overtly write the good news of Jesus that displaces the bad news of the vow you believed. Ellen's vow was, "I must protect my mother and anybody like my mother who feels alone, no matter what it costs me or others, and I must do this for anyone I meet, no matter my own capacity." But the good news of Jesus is, "Jesus can carry the burdens of lonely people; Jesus has many more people than just me to help those people."

If you want to explore identifying and shedding a childhood vow, you will begin by identifying as concretely and specifically as you're able the vow or vows you believe and sift them against the good news of Jesus. You will write the vow out along with the contrasting good news of Jesus. There is something stark and powerful about looking at what you believe that isn't true. Once you see it written, you then repent of the lie that vow caused you to believe and you embrace the good news of Jesus' truth. Like many of these exercises, this will likely not be a one-and-done experience. But you may experience an initial breakthrough of insight by looking at what you believed all these years.

The stories we tell ourselves, idols, and vows. They are intense and entrenched deep into our soul and they keep our false selves fed and animated. When Jesus and Paul invited us to die to self, this is what we're dying to so we can experience the freeing resurrection power of Christ. When Paul warned the church in Galatia to not be bound again by the yoke of slavery, I think this is what he was talking about. Vows and idols are oppressive, but Christ is freeing, and our battle for freedom may be an ongoing battle, but definitely a worthwhile one.

DISCUSSION QUESTIONS

1. What is your reaction to the idea that we all have a "story I tell myself"? Are you able to identify the filter, or inner voice, that is making meaning of your experiences and telling you the way you think the world is?

2. Do you have an example of when you filled in the gap between "what is" and "what you thought is"?

3. Can you name a *same species syndrome* in your life?

4. Are you able to identify any idols in your life? Can you list what you live for when you are not living for Jesus and what you *need* to be okay?

5. Can you write down some of your childhood vows?

6. What effect have your idols and vows had on your well-being?

7. Where do you see the gospel of Jesus displacing the story you tell yourself? How is this freeing for you?

five

SOURCES OF
RELATIONAL ANXIETY

> Chronic anxiety might be compared to the volatile atmosphere of a
> room filled with gas fumes, where any sparking incident could set
> off a conflagration, and where people would then blame the person
> who struck the match rather than trying to disperse the fumes.
> —EDWIN FRIEDMAN

Anxiety isn't as neatly categorized as the chapter headings infer, but some sources of anxiety come from external relationships rather than internal triggers. And external sources can trigger internal anxiety. As in previous chapters, noticing and naming sources is half the battle, because by naming them you flip the power dynamic;

rather than having you in their grip, you are now able to hold them and see them more objectively. The rest of this chapter is devoted to a list of external sources. I have also noted the external sources that have an internal component.

COGNITIVE DISSONANCE

Cognitive dissonance is caused when someone's words and actions do not match, or when someone's words do not match reality. The disconnect between your understanding of reality and either the other person's behavior or his explanation of reality can put you into cognitive dissonance and generate anxiety. Several years ago, my wife, Lisa, and I were getting our coats to walk out the door for a fund-raising banquet that I was hosting. As we were about to leave, the doorbell rang and my mother-in-law, Sue, was at the door with an old friend from out of town. The friend had surprised Sue with a visit, and Sue knew that Lisa would want to catch up with her. Wonderful! Except we were about to leave. So when Lisa saw her mother and friend at the door, it put her into cognitive dissonance because she couldn't match the reality of us walking out the door with now needing to stay and visit. Sue was also caught, as we were very obviously about to leave, so she was apologizing.

Lisa turned to me and asked, "When are you leaving for the fund-raiser?" which was the only way she knew in the moment to manage the situation, but that question put me into dissonance because "we" were very much leaving, not "me." I was unable to nimbly change plans and I replied, "*We* are leaving right now!" which only served to add anxiety to the situation.

If any of us had been able to manage our own anxiety, we could have muddled through. For example, I could have simply replied to my wife, "Actually, I'm walking out right now, I'll see you there."

After all, I needed to be there for a sound check, but Lisa didn't need to be there for another hour. I was unable to clear my head in the moment to help the situation.

Of course, this is a rather benign example—my wife stayed behind and had a lovely visit; I arrived for the sound check. No harm, no foul, but so often we find ourselves anxious because we are unable to process either the circumstance or the message someone is sending because it is incongruent with reality or at least incongruent with our perception of reality. Once you are in dissonance, it is difficult to see reality—in this case that we had more options in that moment than we thought. We all felt "stuck" in rigid options, but we did not actually need to leave together and we had the option to all get what we needed (me to a sound check, the rest of the merry crew catching up for a visit). This case was a comedy of errors as each of us was in cognitive dissonance, unable to guide us to a simple solution.

Cognitive dissonance is very difficult to notice in the moment, but if you find yourself at odds with reality, with someone's behavior, or with his or her perception of reality, it may be that you are in dissonance. At this point you would be wise to pause and reflect on your options. More often, however, you notice *after the fact* that you are in dissonance. As in the above example, it happened, and then we sorted it out. None of us were able to sort it out live.

MIXED MESSAGES

Mixed messages are a specific form of cognitive dissonance. A mixed message is two conflicting messages arriving at the same time from someone. Passive-aggression is a mixed message, so is sarcasm. Sometimes mixed messages don't do any real damage, like good-natured sarcasm between friends, but usually a mixed message from someone will cause significant anxiety. Mixed messages are a form of cognitive dissonance because you cannot process the opposite signals you are receiving in a way that settles your brain. Instead you come away feeling confused or hurt.

In October 1962, John Kennedy gathered with his brother Bobby, his Chief of Staff, and the Chairman of the Joint Chiefs of Staff to make sense of a telex they had received from Nikita Khrushchev of Russia. It was day thirteen of what came to be known as the Cuban Missile Crisis: the Cold War standoff between the United States and Russia. Kennedy was holding a telex that suggested the whole world was about to end.

The problem began two weeks prior when American spy planes discovered Russia was building nuclear missile silos in Cuba. Once they were operational the missiles could reach any target on the East Coast of America, including Washington, DC. For almost two weeks the White House team explored every diplomatic and military option to stop Russia from proceeding, including a huge navy blockade of ships off the Cuban border, but nothing slowed the Russians down. It was the closest the Cold War ever came to an actual war. During a United Nations meeting, US diplomat Adlai Stevenson showed spy plane photos of the nuclear silos, and the Russians flat denied it.

As the crisis escalated, Kennedy received a back-channel communication that Khrushchev would agree to remove the missile silos, and sure enough, several hours later the Oval Office received a telex from the Kremlin confirming that Russia would pull out of Cuba. The crisis was averted, and for the first time in two weeks the White House team slept well, knowing the nuclear threat was over.

The next morning, a second telex from the Kremlin. This one stated that they were *not* going to pull out of Cuba, and that their missiles would be operational within hours. There was no mention of the previous telex received twelve hours before. Two telexes twelve hours apart with completely opposite messages.

Mixed signals cause relational anxiety for the recipient because you don't know which signal to receive and which to reject. Passive-aggressive behavior or certain forms of sarcasm can cause you anxiety, as can the relief from, then threat again, of nuclear war. How do you handle mixed signals, especially when the stakes are impending doom?

Kennedy's advisors kicked around several ideas and finally Bobby Kennedy spoke up. His suggestion: ignore the message we don't want to hear, accept the message we do want to hear, and pretend we never received the second telex. The others were apoplectic. *Pretend we didn't receive the second telex from Khrushchev? What, are we in third grade now?* But it worked. Kennedy sent a telex back thanking Russia for agreeing to remove their missiles, and Russia did. By accepting and acting on the first message and ignoring the second message, they averted nuclear war.

Wait. What? Surely ignoring one message and accepting the preferred one cannot be that simple. This approach comes with no guarantees, but it did avert a nuclear war and became a literal textbook case on the nature of communication (that's where I first read about it). What Bobby Kennedy counted on turned out to be true: maybe the Russians are just as worried as we are; maybe they are looking for a way to peace like we are. So the White House chose the preferred of the two messages, and you can do that as well.

If you find yourself in the anxiety of interpreting mixed messages, simply choose the message you want to receive, ignore the other, and see what happens. The reason this works is twofold. One, it puts the anxiety where it belongs—back on the communicator of the mixed message. Mixed messages cause anxiety because we don't know the intent and meaning, so rather than worry about it, or worse yet, fill in the gaps in our own minds, put the burden of clarity where it belongs: with the original communicator. Two, almost all communication is more fluid than we think.

For all Khrushchev's bluster and complex history with Kennedy (he had given a puppy to Jackie the year before), Khrushchev was still a human who didn't want nuclear destruction. His telex was rigid on two-dimensional paper, but Bobby Kennedy counted on Khrushchev being more nervous and flexible than he appeared, and Bobby was right.

If you work with a concrete thinker or a strong personality, you can mistakenly think that his mode of communication represents his level of commitment to it, but most of the time, we are not as hardened in our messages as we may come across. One way to deescalate anxiety is to simply ask or, in Kennedy's case, act on the preferred message. One of the mistakes we make is we *adopt the presumption of the communicator.* Some people naturally communicate in a rigid way, and their statements are more rigid than they may intend. One way to move communication forward is to not automatically adopt the presumption of the communicator. We cover this more later when we look at reframing.

If you are on the receiving end of cutting sarcasm or a manipulative person who likes messing with you, try receiving the preferred message and ignoring the other and see what happens. Let's take sarcasm as a sample point. Some sarcasm is friendly banter among friends, but some has a knife's edge to it and you can feel the knife go in even when the words are positive. Which message do you want to receive? If you receive the positive words and ignore the knife, it confuses the person being sarcastic toward you. He's thinking, *Does he not realize I'm cutting him?* But it forces the communicator to decide if he is going to strike again.

Sometimes there is wisdom in receiving the knife wound. I've had situations when I can feel the attack even while the person is smiling or using flattering words. Rather than receive the positive message, I intentionally feed back to the communicator that I received the knife wound. I tell him, "Well, if your intent was to hurt me, then well done, you definitely hurt me. I can feel the bleeding." Intentionally choosing to receive the negative message puts the onus back on the message sender. Was his intent really to cut that deep? Passive-aggressive and seasoned sarcastic people often don't realize the impact of their way. Either way, by selecting one message, you put the burden of clarity where it belongs: back on the communicator. If you read her intent wrong, sure enough, she will let you know.

DOUBLE BIND

Christmas morning, the family is gathered around while Ryan opens two gifts from his mother. The two gifts are a red shirt and a blue shirt. They are the same brand, same size, just different colors. He likes them both equally, but later in the day he comes out for dinner wearing the red shirt. His mum asks, "Why didn't you like the blue shirt?"

A double bind is another type of cognitive dissonance in which you find yourself in a situation where no matter what you choose, you lose. It is almost always a two-option scenario, either real or imagined. I say imagined because one aspect of a double bind is the false assumption that there are two options when in fact there may be more. But in the moment, you feel stuck between a rock and a hard place. Double binds are the source of much anxiety in leaders, especially when you don't recognize that you are in one. You spend much energy trying to win when you are set up to lose. Double binds are unique because they are sources of both relational or internal anxiety, depending on the bind.

Relational Double Binds

I spent more than four years working as a crisis care pastor in Las Vegas, one of the most under-resourced cities in the world. Dozens of people every week would come by the church for assistance, and some of them would try to put me in a double bind. A classic example is a person who took me to his car to show me his family and let me know they needed money for rent in the next hour or they would be evicted. Our assistance process for that amount of money was intentionally slow; we had a group that considered all requests and took a few days to respond. People don't discover they are getting evicted the day of eviction; they often have days or even several weeks' notice. The way the man presented the scenario made me feel that I suddenly had to rescue him, when I could not. Don't get me wrong, I wanted to help the family, but the man was offering two options that both involved losing. The specific double bind is some form of, "I need you to provide a simple immediate solution to this long-term, complex problem and no one else but you can help."

Double binds can be insidious. Sometimes you notice them when someone is seeking your help. You listen and as you suggest helpful next steps, the person swats them away and you are trying harder than the person is to help his or her situation. Nothing will work, yet the person expects you to suggest the magic solution that doesn't exist.

Narcissists and psychopaths intentionally use double binds as a form of mental abuse. I know of a department head at a large church who would paint a clear target of where his staff should be leading and then punish them when they hit the target. Classic lose-lose. Family members can unintentionally put each other in double binds. Perhaps your uncle calls and tells you very private information about your cousin and then asks you to act like you don't know. You would normally call your cousin and express concern, but in doing so, you violate the wish of your uncle. Not calling feels coldhearted, especially if your loved one finds out later you've known all along. Double bind.

Internal Double Binds

Some people put themselves in a double bind, which can be especially difficult to notice. If you find yourself agonizing over even the simplest decisions, you might be prone to double binding yourself. One sign that you do this is if you finally make a decision and then spend mental energy regretting that you didn't go the other way. You actually successfully navigated what felt to you like a double bind, but you still punish yourself for what could have been if you made the other decision.

The youth minister at our church has a very wise policy to cancel high school youth group if the roads might be icy at the end of the night. He chooses safety first for these young teen drivers, but one morning after youth group had been cancelled, one of our interns was lamenting that they shouldn't have cancelled youth group after all. The weather that was supposed to show up in force never really arrived. "We should have gone ahead with the meeting," the intern said. That's a double bind.

Putting yourself in lose-lose situations takes an unnecessary amount of emotional and intellectual energy. You can notice when you are putting yourself in a double bind and simply ask yourself, "How much energy do I want to expend on this decision?" Another simple anxiety de-escalation is to weigh the importance of the decision. Some people put themselves in double binds because they agonize over decisions that don't really matter that much either way. If you find yourself anxious, you can pause and reflect on how significant it will be if you "get it wrong."

Getting Out of a Double Bind

The insidious nature of a double bind is the belief there are only two options when often there are more. It is the "locked in" feeling that generates so much anxiety. God offers an open-ended future, but a double bind convinces us that we are backed into a corner of doom. So, a double bind can be another way we live by self rather than faith. God often has a path outside the "two doomed options," and if you're able to pause and reflect on the options, you'll often find many more paths than you first thought. Often you will need the perspective of a trusted friend to help you see the other paths.

Having said that, sometimes we really are in a true double bind: we only have two losing options. When this is truly the case, go ahead and get it over with. I've been in relationships before where the game is, "You lose." The person I am dealing with has no interest in resolution, so no matter what I try, I am always losing. When that is the case, go ahead and lose and move on. You are going to lose a few, and by a few of course I mean a lot. No need to punish yourself when you lose a game of "You lose." Sometimes the best way to manage certain loss is to reframe what a win is. A win is losing quickly, losing well, and moving on. Boom.

PARADOX

A paradox is very similar to a double bind. It is simply an impossible situation where you are trying to do something that is impossible to do. The shortest paradox I know is the command "Be spontaneous!" Having been commanded to suddenly stop whatever you are doing and be spontaneous, you now cannot. Anything you do may appear spontaneous but is not, because of the command. Measuring humility is also a paradox and so is the secret yearnings of many relationships:

"It isn't that I want my child to clean her room. I want her to *want* to clean her room."

"I don't want my husband to pursue me; I want him to *want* to pursue me. I shouldn't have to ask him. He should already *want* to do it."

The most common paradox I encounter as a pastor is the posture of people who send the concurrent message, in various forms, "Come here. Go away." They want help, they don't want help. They want you to care and step in, they want you to back off and leave them alone. Paradox.

Sometimes you can find yourself anxious because of a paradox, either of your own making or of someone else's. Much like a double bind, some people are prone to put themselves into a paradox, and it can be helpful to recognize it. The best solution for a paradox once you recognize it is to simply name it to the person and work on a new approach together that is actually achievable. If the child cleans his room to the parent's satisfaction, regardless of heart intent, that is a win. And for the record, I am a middle-aged man and I still don't want to clean my room. I don't even want to want to, but I clean it all the same.

PHANTOM STRIKES

A phantom strike is anytime one person takes a shot at you, but she is carrying a hidden army with her. It is any variation of "Me and a bunch of people who aren't here and who I won't name all think there is something wrong with you."

Ah, the phantom strike. It is indeed a menace.

Phantom strikes hurt because they are a direct hit, but the weapon has more firepower than you first realized. What you thought was a single bullet turns into a shotgun with all kinds of pellets. Phantom strikes hurt because they catch you when your defense is down; you never see the extra firepower coming. They also hurt because you can't face your accusers square on and now your internal triggers are at work. Is the whole organization talking about me? Are the people who are kind to my face stabbing me in the back? How many people and how strongly do they feel about this? Since you don't have access to any of this information, your mind fills in the gaps, usually to a pathological level, making something potentially much bigger than it really is.

I was hit by a phantom strike several years ago. A man came to confront me about a theological issue he had with my preaching. I was teaching on a matter from Scripture that had many perspectives, but he believed a very narrow perspective was the only possible one. Anyone who explored other options was a heretic. He told me, "Our small group all talked about it and we all agreed that you're out of line." I knew several members of the small group, some of whom I considered friends, and I was hurt that my friends hadn't come to talk to me about it. I called one of them to ask him about it. Full disclosure: before the call, I needed several days to work through my defensiveness and hurt so when I finally called I could ask, very casually, "Hey, Paul said that you have an issue with what I presented in that last sermon. Is that true?"

My friend was immediately defensive, "Oh, that's just Paul. He's always going off on something and I never know what to say. He rants almost every week and I just sort of smile and nod. Don't worry about it. It's just his way."

Don't worry about it. It's just his way. My tombstone could read, "Here lies Steve. He bled out from 'Don't worry about it. It's just his way.'" Of course, as Paul was ranting he was interpreting the smiling and nodding from his group as, "You not only agree, you hold the same level of passion about this that I do."

I had to tell my friend, "Well, Paul is invoking you and everyone in the group as a mob against me." My friend had no idea he was being co-opted into an anti-heresy mob.

People who have strong personalities but don't have emotional maturity to communicate directly are most prone to phantom strikes. They speak boldly against someone and interpret people's silence as agreement, and then co-opt it into a mob. If you've ever received criticism that hurt more than usual it might be because you received a phantom strike.

STEPPING ON A LEADERSHIP LAND MINE

Leadership land mines can really do damage. You're leading a group and you have no idea there are highly emotional topics and history involved in the decision at hand. As you're leading you think all is well, you're even excited, but someone in the group is hurt or highly offended. You've stepped right on a land mine you didn't know existed. Martin is a lead pastor, and he wrote,

> For the fifty years of its existence, this church has never had a woman preach or serve on the board of directors. Two years ago, in private meetings the leadership board of the church began discussing if it was time to make a change regarding women in leadership. Over the time frame of a year we shared our views and opinions. We read books presenting multiple perspectives. Things got a bit heated at times, but in general we listened well. At the end of the year, we came to a consensus that it was time for the church to make a shift. We believe that in our church women should have every opportunity to serve in leadership as men [do].
>
> Part of my job entails working with this leadership board that we call elders. Another part of my job entails leading the paid staff, and these are two separate groups in our organization that don't have a lot of leadership interaction. After the elders made this large decision it was time to tell the staff what we had decided. The elders wrote a lengthy paper explaining why we were making this decision and emailed it to all the staff. We then set up an evening meeting to come together as the elders, staff, and spouses so we could discuss together this transition in our church. The staff was nominally aware the elders were discussing this topic but they had not really grasped the reality of it . . . until the night of that dreaded meeting.
>
> I should have clued into the anxiety in the room when I walked in and it was quiet . . . like crickets quiet! No one had touched the cute cheese and meat plates we put out. There were only perfunctory salutations followed by a lot of awkward silence. I started the meeting and the guns came out quickly. I was taken aback. How could my very staff not be in alignment with the elders? How could

a group who was generally cohesive now start forming little circles and begin throwing stones at the others? How could I be so unaware and out of touch with many on my staff?

I had stepped on a land mine I didn't even know was there. In the moment, I wanted to throw stones too. I wanted to blame and point fingers. Fortunately, I did not do that. What I did do was close the meeting out as peacefully as possible and then took some time to reflect on what had happened. Instead of blaming others for their actions, I began to see how my actions had caused much of the turmoil. I had greatly underestimated how important this issue is to some people. While the elders were afforded a year of debate, study, and discussion in coming to a decision, I had given none of that to the staff. I had stepped on a land mine that was much more deeply embedded than I was aware, but I also added TNT to it in the way I approached the situation.

Leadership land mines are particularly tricky because everyone loses a leg in the explosion. The people receiving the new direction are hurt, but so is the leader who feels shame for not seeing it coming. The impact can be significant relational anxiety. Like many of these sources, the best way to diffuse the issue is to name it, in the moment if you're able. You cannot undo the damage, but you can diffuse the anxiety by naming it and inviting people to share their point of view and assumptions. You can share yours as well and move through the situation together.

POWER AND RESPONSIBILITY

Another source of relational anxiety is when you are serving in a role where your responsibility and power do not match. You are constantly in an anxious state, but you cannot put your finger on the source. It may be because you are responsible for significant aspects of your organization, but you've not been given the authority to manage your responsibility. If you find yourself "in trouble" for a decision that impacts your work or you have to clean up a mess not of your making, it may be because you have responsibility but no power.

A young pastor accepts a lead role at a flagship church where the founding pastor is still serving. As much as the founder speaks of excitement over the new pastor's arrival, he is not ready to hand over power. The new pastor is left with all responsibility and little actual power.

An interim pastor is asked to bridge the gap between the previous pastor, who had a moral failing, and the next pastor the church is yet to find. The interim is asked to help deal with systemic issues, but every time he tries, he is shut out. All responsibility, no power.

A woman marries a decent man who still talks to his mother every week. No matter what the wife wants, the mother gets what she wants. The mother has no responsibility and lots of power, and the wife has responsibility but little actual power.

Some people have control issues, some don't know how to delegate. Some are threatened by systemic change. Whatever the reason, if you have much responsibility but no power to execute, you will battle ongoing anxiety until that dynamic changes or until you leave.

TRIANGULATION

A triangulated relationship is any three-person relationship that should have two people in it. This isn't to be confused with a three-person relationship that should have three people in it! A healthy three-person relationship might be a father, mother, and daughter who all relate together. A triangulated version of that relationship is where the daughter says, "Don't tell Dad" or the father says to the daughter, "I'll let you do it, but your mum is going to hit the roof. You know how she can be." A triangulated relationship is where two people collude against the third or one person co-opts an outsider into a two-person relationship. Gossip is always a form of triangulation, as are most middle school relationships. Picture the following twelve-year-olds talking about a crush: "Jenny asked me to tell you that she likes you. Do you like her back? I'll go back and tell her if you do." Next time tell Jenny that I don't do triangulated relationships and she can talk to me herself, said no middle schooler ever.

Triangles can be especially deadly in leadership because they add unnecessary drama and anxiety into relationships. But they can also get you triangled into a situation and you may not even be aware of it. Have you ever had someone vent to you about another person and you just listened? Depending on the character of the person, he or she may take your caring listening as agreement and collusion. Next thing you know, a friend is calling you upset.

"Dana told me that you and her were talking about me and you both think I have a problem."

"Wait, I was just listening to Dana, trying to be kind. I don't have a problem with you at all!"

You do now, brother.

People who struggle with direct communication are particularly prone to triangulation because co-opting people onto their "team" is a way they overcome their feeling of powerlessness. They recruit, sometimes well-intentioned, oftentimes not, trying to get a gang against the person with whom they have an issue. Rather than speak directly to the person, they speak about him or her to everyone else. Beware secret knowledge, both sharing it and being invited into it. Unless you're dealing with a confidential counseling-type appointment, secret knowledge is almost always a form of triangulation.

Jay Haley was one of the early adopters of family systems theory, and he coined the phrase, "perverse triangle," which is when a parent treats one of her or his children like a spouse. Perhaps a husband is not giving the emotional care to his wife that she needs, so she begins depending on her oldest son for it: asking his advice, even about her marriage to his dad, crying to him when she's upset. This is a particularly difficult triangle to detangle because it involves hurting a mother you love.

The Bible shows many triangled relationships. You can get all the examples you need just by looking at Abraham and his family. Take Jacob for example: Jacob, Esau, and Rebekah were a triangle in which Rebekah and Jacob colluded against Esau to steal his blessing. Also, Jacob, Laban, and Rachel exemplified a triangled relationship. Not to mention Jacob, Rachel, and Leah. Come to think of it, Jacob plus any two people inevitably formed a triangle. No wonder Jacob was always in the center of drama. But not just Jacob; you don't have to spend too much time with Abraham before you run into triangulated relationships between he, Sarah, Hagar, Ishmael, and Isaac.

The simplest way to get out of a triangled relationship is to inform everybody that you are going to inform everybody. Give everybody the same access to the same information. I have had instances where I say, "You have twenty-four hours to tell them and then I am going to." Again, the exception is for those of us whose role requires confidentiality, but even then, you must proceed with extreme caution. Let's say Kathy came in to talk to you about Jim. She wants you to talk to Jim about issues she has with him. Beware. Triangle. Better for Kathy to bring Jim in and say, "Here's what I told the pastor. I want him to help us." If not, and you call Jim, you do damage. Also, if you know something about Jim, but he does not know that you know, and you use that knowledge, even in a well-meaning way, you can potentially cause damage. Please, pastors and faith leaders, if you have "secret" knowledge about someone that someone else told you, don't call the person and say, "The Holy

Spirit told me." And if you were thinking, "Well, I *think* the Holy Spirit used this person to tell me," then at least have the honesty to say so. If someone asks me to call a loved one and offer to help them, I first say, "I'll happily call. Here is what I am going to tell them. 'Kathy asked me to call you because she is concerned about you and she wants me to help.'" No secret knowledge, no relating based on triangled information.

All these relational sources can be extra challenging because the solution to them almost always involves engaging the person you're anxious about. Dealing with internal anxiety can be a private matter, but the best way to reduce relational anxiety is to address it with the people you are in tension with. On most occasions, if you have trust and respect, this will go well. But if you don't trust the people, or if they are toxic, you may not be safe to deal with them directly about it. That is why your anxiety continues—because you do not have an outlet for it. In those cases, you may need to take a more drastic measure, such as asking someone safe to join the conversation, but again, no triangulating. Just admit you needed help from a third party for your own sake not simply to gang up on them.

I was wrapping up the writing of this chapter when I noticed a pattern in my preteen daughter's television habits. The shows she loves involve all the concepts in this chapter. A lightbulb lit up in my head: no wonder they call that genre a "drama." No wonder my daughter gets caught up in the plot and the relationships and can't wait for the next episode; they almost always end the episode with unresolved relational tension. Triangles, double binds, paradoxes, and mixed messages galore. The writers of the shows were using these very sources of anxiety to keep people hooked to the shows, and it worked! But our goal is to keep the drama on the television for entertainment and keep the healthy relationships in the real world for all our sakes.

DISCUSSION QUESTIONS

1. How is relational anxiety different for you from internal anxiety? Is one easier to deal with than the other?
2. Which of the sources above do you most struggle with? What does that look like in your life?
3. Can you give some examples from above when you were in relational anxiety?
4. Are you able to name any sources of external anxiety that are not listed in this chapter?
5. Can you share a time when you dealt with relational anxiety alongside someone? When is a time it went well? When did it not go so well?
6. When you are in tension with someone, how does that add to your anxiety load? What do you do to reduce it? How do you stay connected with that person?

six

APPLYING FAMILY SYSTEMS TO LEADERSHIP

*All that is necessary to create an emotional
system is spending time together.*
—ROBERTA GILBERT

To get to the other side of anxiety and experience genuine freedom, we make the courageous move from diagnosis to action.
Self-awareness is a great start, but true freedom comes in forging a
new path and moving into a new reality. The preceding chapters are
all designed to help you think about the way you think, to move from
a generalized feeling to an acute diagnosis of what is causing your
anxiety. Self-awareness alone will not bring about healthy change. We
all know people who are self-aware and obnoxious. They are some

version of "I am what I am and that is the way it is." What we are
going for is way beyond self-awareness; it is systemic health. Thinking
about the way you think is one thing. Bravely forging a new path with
vulnerability and openness is an altogether different level.

Jesus obviously brought a revolution when he came to earth. One
particular revolution we overlook is how he forever shifted our perspective of health and infection. Before Jesus, if someone was sick or
sinful, people believed that person's body or soul was corrupt, and
healthy people had to avoid him or her at all costs. People such as
lepers had to steer clear, and some even wore bells to warn you of
their presence so you wouldn't come into close proximity with them.
In the same way, religious leaders avoided "sinners," so their holiness wouldn't be polluted. But Jesus came along and blew that whole
operation up. He touched lepers and disease-ridden people; he associ-
ated with "sinners" and enjoyed their company.

Jesus forever changed the perception of infection and sin transfer.
When Jesus, the healthy and holy man, touched the sick and when
he lived in close proximity to "sinners," he infected them. Instead of
Jesus becoming sick or sinful, the people became clean. The writer
of Proverbs and 1990s youth leaders everywhere tell us that "bad
company corrupts good character" (1 Cor. 15:33), and of course that
can be true, but Jesus brought a more powerful truth. Now, because
of Jesus: "Greater is he that is in you, than he that is in the world"
(1 John 4:4 KJV). He showed us the incredible power of the gospel—
that health can infect ill health, rather than the other way around.

Family systems theory has a similar power available to it. A healthy
leader can move into a "sick" system and slowly move it toward health.
With a few systems tools under a leader's belt, she can reduce chronic
anxiety and break chronic patterns, creating a culture of health for
people to get well. The higher up in an organization a leader is, the
more power that leader has to create health. The converse is also true:
if the top leader is chronically unhealthy, the whole system suffers. A

lower-level leader may create health for her team, but will struggle to thrive in the overall organization. The principle that "health infects ill health" remains true and provides great hope for a leader trying to move an organization, a family, or system.

A system is simply a group of people who function in an emotional unit. Because everyone in the system is interconnected (connected to one another and affected by one another's connections), a system becomes a complex environment that generates a lot of emotional subtext, especially if one member of the system is unhealthy or disruptive. Systems become anxious when members of a system adopt and escalate one another's anxiety and reactivity. System leadership is a developed skill where the leader pays as much attention to the system dynamic as she does to conversation. A leader who pays attention to a system isn't so much concerned with the content of what is said, but rather the process of how people are relating and behaving. Systems get stuck in predictable patterns and a skilled leader can break through this "stuckness" by paying attention to relational patterns and help his people detangle and break free.

> *A leader who pays attention to a system isn't so much concerned with the content of what is said, but rather the process of how people are relating and behaving.*

PROCESS VERSUS CONTENT

The first step in systems thinking is paying attention to the way people are relating (process) while also listening to what is said (content). We naturally spend most of our time focusing on content even though we frequently *react* to process, so it will take some practice to build your process muscle. A leader gains significant traction by elevating her awareness of process and then leading at the process level. If you've ever seen a news anchor with an earpiece listening to the producer while being able to read the news, it is a bit like that. A process-focused leader will not neglect content, but will add a concurrent layer of awareness: the capacity to notice systemic issues while engaging content.

Most of us already react subconsciously to process dynamics, we just don't naturally pay keen attention to them or name them. The ability to notice systems, dynamics, and recurring patterns is a learned skill, not a gifting or a personality trait, so anybody can do it with some training and practice. Not unlike going to the gym, anyone can exercise his or her process muscle and make great strides, it just may take a few hundred reps to see progress. Here is what leading at a process level can look like and why it can be so powerful:

My sons like to play competitive basketball, and they both play for their school. Several years ago my youngest son came home from practice frustrated that William wasn't passing him the ball. My son is big on justice, and William was violating his sense of justice. William must be punished. My son was twelve.

"William is a ball hog. He never passes the ball to anyone and Coach lets him get away with it."

"What do you do when William doesn't pass?"

"William doesn't pass to me, so I've stopped passing to him."

This is process: not what William and my son said to each other, although no doubt that was not helping, but the *dynamic* between them. They were in a larger system and they were affecting it. The system was the whole team, including the coach. This is the way systems work: their dynamic directly involved two people but indirectly affected every person in the system. Their dynamic had gotten into a chronic, predictable pattern that had caused the system to get stuck. The team sport of basketball had changed because two of the team members were no longer playing basketball, they were playing keep away. They were no longer keeping score of baskets, they were keeping score of who is passing to whom. At this point, content was almost irrelevant; process had taken over and was causing damage, and like many stuck systems, their pattern had become predictable. This is a simple way you can begin to flex your process muscle: begin to pay attention to stuck patterns in your life or in relationships. Some of you know marriages like this. The couple fights all the time, but they always fight *the same way*. The topic of their fight changes but their *pattern of fighting stays the same*. Predictably the same; chronically the same. Stuck.

When a system is stuck, more content is rarely the answer. My son and William would not be able to talk their way through this problem; in fact, talking would have entrenched them deeper into the problem. By applying systemic change, by focusing on process as much as content, you can bring massive change to an organization or family, or in this case a basketball team. One of the reasons is because systems theory echoes the gospel in its power for health to infect ill health. The miracle of systemic change is that it does not require everyone in the system to agree, or even be aware of the problem. You only need the person motivated to change to be willing to change the system. When a system is stuck, one disrupter is all that is required to break free and potentially heal the problem.

My son was the motivated change agent. Actually, if he were writing this he would more accurately say, "I didn't want to change at all, but dear old Dad is a systems fanatic and won't let me complain about a teammate. He made me try some weird systems jujitsu move." But for the sake of this case study, my son was the motivated change agent. So in summary:

The problem: William doesn't pass to my son.

My son's attempted solution to the problem: punish William by not passing to him.

The chronic, predictable pattern that gets the system stuck: William and my son withhold the ball from each other because each thinks the other is a ball hog. Now two players are no longer working as a team and the team score is suffering for it.

One of the most critical aspects of "content versus process" is taking the time to get to the bottom of the process problem. What *exactly* is the problem and what *exactly* is the attempted solution, and what does the stuck process look like? If you're feeling stuck with someone or with a group, your first step is to pay attention to the process, but your second vital step is to map out the pattern like I did with the basketball dilemma above. If your marriage is stuck in a predictable fighting pattern, you can sit down together and map out not what you fight about but the way you fight. Who starts it? Who escalates? Who backs away in retreat? Who needs space for resolution, and who needs immediate closure? Of course, if you try this and end up fighting about the way you fight in the same way you fight about everything else, then maybe that is a signal to find a person outside your system to help.

Just so we understand each other, you are often a significant part of the problem that got the system stuck, and so am I. Even though I have studied and practiced systems theory for years, I am still in a system, therefore still part of the problem. Many leaders have an ego that can blind them to their own contribution to the problem. In this basketball case my son was speaking like a victim, but he was contributing to the stuckness. I am sure that William was going home to his family saying the exact same thing my son told me, except in William's version he was the victim and my son was the perpetrator! This is often what keeps us stuck: the inability to see our own culpability in a system. The need to see ourselves always as the victims of someone else's behavior.

Mature leaders can see their own contributions, which makes them powerful agents of systemic health. Unfortunately for my son his parents are trained in family systems theory and are hyper aware of process. I'm sure my kids sometimes wonder why they can't have normal parents who hear about an annoying teammate and say, "That's too bad, William must be a jerk." Instead they get this:

"If you want William to pass the ball more, pass the ball to him the next six times you have the ball. Even when someone else is open, don't pass to them, pass to William the next six times."

"But that's not fair. That's rewarding his ball-hog ways. He should be the one to pass the ball first."

My son was initially reactive because he was telling me this story for sympathy, also known as "recruiting me onto his team." But as his dad I am permanently, unwaveringly, unconditionally on his team. That doesn't mean I collude with him against the "villain" William. As I suggested a systemic change, my son got anxious because I was putting pressure on the story he was telling himself. Part of systemic change is learning to be a nonanxious presence in a highly anxious environment. More on that toward the end of the chapter.

I told my son, "For the next six times you have the ball, I'm going to ask you to trust me and pass William the ball. It will change everything."

To my son's great credit, because he is unfailingly courteous and respectful, he did just that. He didn't like it and he didn't believe in it, but he did it. Sure enough, after several passes William passed the ball back, the pattern was permanently changed, and they went from enemies to friends even outside the court. Their problem went away without ever talking about it or without the coach getting involved. They never dealt on a content level. The systemic stuckness simply dissolved. This is the power of systems-level leadership.

Of course, not all stuck processes have a Disney ending like this. Sometimes they get worse, especially if you are dealing with sabotage, or you are bringing change to a system that has been stuck for a long time. After twenty years of marriage, suddenly no longer picking up after your spouse a few times will likely not change his or her entrenched habit of leaving a mess. After a church has "always done it this way" for a decade and gone through three pastors who attempted to bring needed change, a quick systemic analysis is not going to do it.

In the basketball example, the system had only been stuck for a couple of weeks. Also, while the system had twelve people in it, only two were stuck, so this was a small and simple systemic issue that had not been stuck long.

If you are in a system that has been stuck for years, or a system that has many people in it, systemic change will be much slower and more painful, but the approach is exactly the same. Many leaders who bring systemic health and change to a very stuck church might take a few years. The change agent may become a scapegoat if enough people in the system sabotage his efforts. There are many variables. The outcome may take longer, be more painful, and require multiple solutions to multiple systemic issues. On the other hand, if a number of leaders are aware of what is stuck or sick and all are willing to change it, significant change and health can come much quicker.

So for those situations, once you have mapped out the process problem, your next move might be to recruit people to help with the process change so you have more leadership horsepower applying the systemic change. I do not offer this as a magic formula or something easy—process-level leadership takes courage and time—but many times I have experienced its miraculous ability to dissolve a long-standing issue that was unresolvable through content-only focus.

What about a situation more complex with more at stake? Maybe you're a church leader with a difficult board or a sensitive pastor transition. Maybe you're a parent trying to navigate the moods and whims of your teen or interfering in-law. What then? While the situation is more complex and therefore might be slower to change, the approach is the same. First try to name the dynamic of what is going on. Spend less time on content and more time on the pattern that is recurring and stuck. The more specific you can name the pattern, the more chance of true change. Next, see if you can identify your attempted solutions to the pattern. If you want to see quicker process change, bring all the parties into the discussion. In other words, name the dynamic with the people involved. Note: the absolute magic sauce of this is the capacity to name the dynamic without heat in your words. I have led many process-level changes where I first had to work on my own reactivity before proceeding, sometimes taking days or even weeks to get into a nonreactive place to be able to lead a group through change. Leading a productive, nonanxious conversation about a difficult or sensitive topic is essential to process-level change. Remember, *people pay attention to content but react to process,* so you'll have to be prepared for an anxious response and your ability to be nonanxious will be key.

Finally, your ability to change the system will be dependent on several factors, one of which is the willingness of the others in the system to move toward health. If you are a young pastor leading a traditional church board, set your stopwatch for a few years. It is going to take time and some allies and therefore some stamina.

Over years of teaching this material to all ages in various cultures, I have discovered that anybody can notice process as much as content. You may take a while to build your process muscle, but over time you can notice patterns, and most powerfully, you can notice how you are contributing to the stuck patterns that frustrate you. If you lead out of process as much as content you will become a much more powerful leader.

PROBLEM FORMATION AND PROBLEM RESOLUTION

In the example above, I allude to "attempted solutions." Understanding the nature of how problems are formed and how they are resolved will help you tremendously in process thinking. All people have problems. But how do problems become chronic to the point that you get stuck? Family systems theorists teach that our own attempted solutions often make problems worse. Have you found yourself in a difficult situation with someone you're leading and your best effort to resolve the problem only makes the problem worse? That is because most solutions are what family systems theorists call "first-order change." To permanently break a toxic pattern, you need to access "second-order change."

One of the signs that an attempted solution is making a situation stuck is when the result of your attempt is more of the same. This is first-order change. As you notice process and map out stuck patterns, one internal red flag you can watch for is "more of the same." If you are attempting to solve a problem with "more of the same," you can be assured that you are making the problem more entrenched. Some examples of "more of the same" are: try harder, sacrifice even more for that person, give even more insight than you did before so he will understand, worry more about him. Just keep doing more of what isn't working now and you will entrench a systemic problem into stuckness and your system will increase in anxiety.

A single father once came in for a pastoral meeting. His wife had died seven years earlier, and his problem was his twelve-year-old son's increasing need for affection. When he was watching a football game, his preteen son would sit on his lap and hug him. This was particularly difficult when Dad's friends were over for a beer. The father tried to tell his son various forms of the message "real men don't express open affection." The father also sent nonverbal cues of embarrassment to his son. The more the dad told the son to "man up" and pushed him away, the more clingy the son got. The dad was only making first-order change because he tried an attempted solution that made the situation worse, and then he applied "more of the same."

Let's map out the process. The problem in this case was two inter-related problems: a son's need for physical affection and the father's discomfort with the son's need for affection. Both the father and son were applying an attempted solution. The son's attempted solution was getting physical affection from his nonaffectionate father since he was no longer able to get it from his late mum. Dad's attempted solution was verbal and nonverbal communication of "real men don't do this." Both attempted solutions made the system predictable and stuck.

Second-order change happens when a person is able to recognize that he is stuck in a predicable, chronic pattern. Another way it happens is when at least one person in a stuck or anxious system gets fed up or is in enough pain to seek outside help from someone, such as a therapist or, in this particular case, a pastor at a local church.

When the father came to see me, he and his son had been in this escalating pattern for a few years. Dad could tolerate the physical affection immediately after his wife died, and even when his son was younger, but now that his son was "becoming a man," Dad's anxiety about the problem escalated enough for him to seek help. And yes, of course, I do not agree with the dad's assessment of what a man is, or if his son should have sought affection, but that is an important piece to this. Many people address problems with content. You may be reading this case thinking, *If the father would have come to me, I would have told him that he should get past his prejudice and assumptions and give the son the care he needs.* That solution, which may work, is content level. It is not wrong or bad, but powerful change happens at process level. Convincing Dad to think differently, or that his thinking is wrong, likely will not break the toxic pattern. The pattern requires a process solution known as second-order change.

One method of delivering second-order change is reversing the dynamic. That is why my son's ball-passing problem dissolved—we applied a reversal. His attempted solution was "don't pass," so we applied "pass every time" for a while and the problem dissolved.

Another option is to prescribe the problem. In the father's case, the problem was openly expressed affection, so the prescription became openly expressed affection. I coached the father to pursue the son with openly expressed affection several times per week. "Prescribe the problem" can be trickier to think through, so here it is for this particular case: son is giving too much affection (problem) so father must give too much affection to son (prescribe the problem). Not only was he to practice overcoming his own internal discomfort at his son's behavior, he was to seek out his son and give hugs, rub his head, kiss him on the cheek, tell him he loves him. Part of the problem was the son had to do all the initiating of affection to get what he needed. Because Dad was recoiling, the son did "more of the same" to the point that as a young teen, he was sitting on his dad's lap during football games. By prescribing the problem, we were dissolving the stuck pattern because not only was the dad providing needed affection, he was also *initiating* it multiple times per week.

You might imagine it took some coaching to convince the father to try this, but to his credit, he acknowledged his own solutions were not working and he was game to try anything. One reason he was game is that I let him in on this first-order/second-order change theory. Part of a leader's vocation is equipping people, and once you get the hang of this, you can get further faster by helping your team understand this approach. The prescription immediately dissolved the stuck system and began to not only build a new healthy system, but it actually served the added bonus of dissolving the son's problem. The son no longer had to pursue his father when he felt starved for affection because his father was now pursuing him. When the son came in for a hug or a cuddle, the dad received it. Also, Dad realized that his assumptions about male affection were not true and that by expressing affection to his son, he was not making his son soft. He became able to express affection to his son even in front of his friends. At the risk of overstating the power of this process approach, the dad was now modeling for his friends what healthy father-son relationships can be. This is the power of a systems focus. Counselors use these techniques all the time, but they are available to prudent leaders as well.

I was recently in a coaching appointment with a church leadership team of four people, and I noticed a recurring pattern during our time together that one guy never spoke unless he was called on to speak. The others would freely share, but he always waited for me or the lead pastor to ask what he thought. Every time he spoke up, he shared pure, succinct wisdom. He was robbing the team of wisdom because of his reticence to speak. I gently invited the team to consider this dynamic that we were all allowing this guy to remain quiet unless called upon. I asked the quiet guy what he thought about this dynamic and he shared, vulnerably, some reasons why he stayed quiet. His team had had no idea because they had never given voice to process before. They had all *noticed* that he was quiet, because almost all of us notice and react to process, but they had never named that he was quiet because they weren't sure how to do it. After talking through the dynamic in a nonanxious way, I asked if he'd be willing to try something.

For the next three meetings, he would share a thought six times without being asked first. He could use the six times any time he wanted, so maybe he'd simply initiate two thoughts per meeting for all three meetings, or if he was nervous, he could wait one whole meeting and do all six in the next meeting to get it over with. He held all the power and choice of when to apply the solution. Further, he was to not only initiate, but on at least two occasions out of the six, he was to interrupt someone while he or she was speaking. People on the team got quite a laugh out of "Mr. Quiet" suddenly interrupting them. The team was game to try this and as we dialed in the plan, Mr. Quiet asked me in front of the others, "Do I have to stay on the same topic, or can I do any interruption?" We all agreed that he could interrupt to discuss a favorite movie or his shopping list or a sports score. Again, content was not as critical as breaking the process.

So let's review. The problem was not that he didn't speak up, the problem was that he did not feel worthy of speaking and didn't feel that he had the power to speak into the group. Speaking was just the manifestation of his deeper problem. Mr. Quiet's attempted solution was to stay quiet. The prescription in this case was two tools: a "reversal" that we have already covered and also applying an absurdity. The process level was that he felt underpowered and under-confident, which is why in the "prescription" we intentionally gave him options with power. He could choose when to apply the solution. He had power over when he'd use his six interruptions and what his topic would be, so he could quietly summon the courage to speak, knowing he didn't have to say the right thing or even say something related to the discussion. This absurdity works because everyone is in on it—now the whole system was invested in making sure Mr. Quiet spoke. It also works because one of Mr. Quiet's issues was confidence and absurdity helped lower his anxiety in trying to speak up more. It wasn't an anxious experience because of the absurdity of the rules— they may be discussing a staff initiative and he could interrupt with the basketball score. It's funny. So reversals, prescribing the problem, and absurdity are three powerful tools to help break a stuck pattern. And as for the prescription of six times—it is just coincidental that it was the same amount as my son's basketball prescription. Six times is an arbitrary number, but enough times to break the stuck pattern.

Leading at a process level brings health and change, sometimes in an immediate breakthrough, sometimes slowly over time. The best thing about process-level leadership is it now gives a leader powerful tools to address chronic frustration. Do you find a particular staff member dif-ficult? Does your team make the same mistakes over and again? Rather than staying frustrated or doing more of the same thing that isn't work-ing, you can pause, pay attention to process, and map out the specific pattern that is occurring. Once you have it mapped out, you can get others involved and prescribe a solution. A reversal or a "prescribe the problem" may do the trick, but if you're struggling with that, you can simply introduce something that changes the pattern. The leader holds the most power in a system, so when the leader is also the motivated change agent the results can be immediate. Also, a healthy leader will always invite her team into this noticing, mapping out the pattern, and second-order change application. The reason the man who was reticent to speak up will likely be comfortable sharing more is the whole team was in on noticing, mapping, and applying a solution. Nothing behind another's back, no manipulation, no condescending approaches, just openly discussed process.

Of course, systems are not automatically toxic. Many relational systems are healthy and keep people in strong bonds. If you've been at someone's home that has much laughter around the dinner table, you're witnessing an example of a healthy recurring pattern. This is why you can often get a feel for a team culture, or why you enjoy being with a particular group of people.

While I have a lot of experience in systems thinking, I am ultimately in my own system and cannot always see second-order change or the way I am contributing to the problems. So I set for myself a low threshold before I reach out for help. For me, a fellow pastor, who is not at my church, or a therapist is able to help me break some chronic patterns and ways of thinking. Often, I ask my own team to help notice it and map it out. This is difficult work but is more fruitful and freeing than "more of the same" and certainly more potent than focusing only on content. You are already reacting to process, you may as well harness that power for real, second-order change.

SECOND-ORDER CHANGE
AND THE GOSPEL

This whole dynamic of problems and attempted solutions is exactly the story of the gospel. I think the gospel must be true, not just because of the historical and philosophical evidence, but also because of the psychological evidence. When Scripture authors talked about sin and Jesus' death breaking sin's power, they were saying the same thing as the family systems experts: our problems are entrenched by our own attempted solutions. We all sin and we all apply attempted solutions to our sin. Scripture says our most common attempted solutions are hiding and blaming. The human solution to sin is more of the same. We are all doomed to this first-order change until a second-order change agent outside our system comes along. Our exploration of Paul's theology of the cross in chapter 2 is the true second-order change that the gospel offers us. We are no longer stuck in a system of sin, we are now free and in a healthy system. Jesus infects our ill health with health.

UNDERFUNCTIONING AND OVERFUNCTIONING RELATIONSHIPS

If you are a high-functioning leader and you love to be helpful, you can fall into the chronic pattern of overfunctioning while the other person underfunctions. If you are a perfectionist and struggle to let others do something because you do it better, you're prone to overfunctioning. One of the simplest changes you can bring to a system is to notice who overfunctions and who underfunctions. Overfunctioners believe the fallacy, "If I just do it one more time for them, they will catch on." Underfunctioners carry private shame of not being able to manage the same capacity or, in rare cases, intentionally underfunction simply to enjoy watching the overfunctioners scurry around doing it all.

Lonesome Dove was a 1980s miniseries featuring two retired Texas Rangers: Augustus "Gus" McCrae and Woodrow F. Call. After thirty years of friendship they had very much developed an overfunctioning and underfunctioning relationship. They ran a small ranch and

Woodrow was constantly working hard. Gus, on the other hand, spent most of his time either visiting the local prostitute or sitting on the porch drinking whiskey and reading the Bible. After a particularly grueling session trying to tame a bucking horse, Woodrow dismounted and stormed over to Gus grumbling that Gus should do more of the work. Gus's reply captured an overfunctioning and underfunctioning relationship perfectly: "I'm just tryin' to keep everything in balance, Woodrow. You do more work than you got to, so it's my obligation to do less." If you are frustrated at a team member who is not pulling his weight and your solution is to pick up the slack, you will only entrench the problem. You are practicing more of the same.

RESISTANCE TO SYSTEMIC CHANGE

Plenty of books have been written about resistance to change. As you incorporate process-level leadership you will encounter resistance, because any group has self-interest to stay the same. Here are three forms of resistance you can expect as you lead.

Sabotage

Most stuck systems will work hard to maintain status quo in the face of a change agent, and one of the most common forms of resistance is sabotage. Ed Friedman pointed out that sabotage has less to do with the content of change and more to do with the leader's initiative.[1] The people causing sabotage are unable to regulate their own anxiety and, worse yet, especially in Christian cultures the group or system will often join the saboteur because it feels like empathy. It is, in fact, appeasement, and a nonanxious leader will need to skillfully keep saboteurs from forming a gang against them. Sabotage is an anxious reaction to an unknown future and any leader can expect it, even from team members they trust. Of course, if you have led an organization for a long time you are at high risk of sabotaging a newer leader's ideas or initiatives, not because her ideas are bad or wrong but because you feel threatened. Paying attention to and noticing sabotage is an effective way to limit its power, but it will always be present when leading systemic change.

Scapegoating

Scapegoating is a form of sabotage and doesn't need much explanation. In the face of change, a group will typically project an issue onto a person to avoid its own contribution to it. In the Old Testament people laid hands on the head of a goat to transmit their sins onto the goat and then cast the goat out into the desert as payment for their sins. Scapegoating happens most in systems where an individual cannot differentiate against the anxiety of a group. Interim leaders and leaders in a revolving door of an organization are especially vulnerable to scapegoating, especially those who have been called in to help an organization identify systemic issues.

If you know of a church that churns through pastors, the problem is usually not the pastor. The incoming leader shows the existing team some issues they need to address to move to health; next thing you know the interim leader is thanked, maybe even prayed over at the end, and then sent out never to be heard from again. That's how you know that final prayer was not a prayer of blessing, it was the casting out of a scapegoat. You now carry the blame of the organization out into the desert, never to be heard from again. A note to a leader who is leaving a church that is toxic: beware if congregates lay hands on you when they pray—they may be transmitting their sins onto you!

Imaginative Gridlock

Imaginative gridlock is a symptom of stuckness and a particular form of "more of the same" where an organization gets stuck because it is trying more of the same to an approach that is already not working. Sometimes the gift of a trusted outsider can kick us out of rigid thinking. When we built our church, we knew our lobby would be too small, but it was all we could afford on our very tight budget. After four years of rapid growth, we found ourselves looking for extra space to squeeze out of our lobby and kept looking at how we could expand our prep room to form a cafe with a bar people could sit at. We paced around, taped off areas, and looked at all manner of options. During that time we hired an executive pastor who had been with the church for a decade before moving away for work. After four years away, he came back to serve on staff. As we explained our lobby efforts he asked, "Why don't you flip the nursery and kitchen?" Our nursery was on one side of our lobby, and the space around it was not well used. By flipping our design, we got everything we wanted—an expanded cafe that fronted a wonderful porch area and a nursery that would serve parents and babies well. The fact is, I would likely have never gotten us to this solution because I was applying "more of the same" to a rigid set of questions. We were stuck in gridlock until Tom came along and ignored the premise of our question including, "How do we expand our prep room" to form a whole new set of questions, including "how do we move elements of this lobby to better fit what we need?"

If you find yourself stuck in sorting through a leadership problem, you can pay attention to the symptoms. The primary symptom is when you keep seeking new answers to old questions rather than reframing the questions. But more subtle symptoms can also reveal gridlock: When your people are easily offended or looking for offense. When there is a lack of playfulness and laughter and an overabundance of earnestness. If your language is either/or, black and white, all-or-nothing thinking that shrinks possibilities into narrow, even doomed options and false dichotomies. If you are struggling to break through with a problem that keeps repeating, rather than trying harder to solve the problem, you can step back and see if you are in imaginative gridlock. If so, you can call on some of your more creative, out-of-the-box thinkers and resource them (with money or permission) to help you get unstuck.

DIFFERENTIATION

Every time you fly an attendant asks you to put down whatever you are doing so you can pay attention while he or she recites a very specific pair of sentences: "In the unlikely event that we lose cabin pressure, masks will drop from the ceiling. *First place the mask over your own face before helping others*" (emphasis added). Why do attendants say that every flight? The legal department surely has something to do with it, but I also think it is because we have to go against our instinct when trouble strikes us and our loved ones. Every parent on that plane needs reminding that she cannot help another if she herself is unconscious, so attendants instruct us to go against what we want to do, get ourselves in the oxygen masks, and then help others. The repetition of hearing it every flight slowly changes the way we think about helping in an anxious situation. This is why a doctor serving on the hospital code team with me said, "When someone's heart stops, first check your own pulse." Of course, he didn't literally stop to make sure he was alive, but he did take note of his own well-being as paddles and commands and "Clear!" were hurling back and forth.

So many leaders struggle with self-care, or get sucked into the next crisis, or carry people's problems, but making sure you are well is the first fundamental step in bringing any systemic change. According to Ed Friedman, the path to systemic change is for a leader to work on "their own integrity and the nature of their own presence rather than techniques for manipulating or motivating others."[2] This is a fascinating and bold theory. If leaders truly want change, working on their own composure will bring about more change than trying to get others to do something. This is known as *differentiation* and it is the most foundational tool for this entire book and yet can be the most difficult to grasp. Roberta Gilbert calls it the "cornerstone concept" because it is what all healthy leadership is built upon.[3]

Differentiation is the ability to be fully yourself while being fully connected to people. It is gaining clarity on where "I" end and the "other" begins. A differentiated person allows space between herself and another, even when that other person is highly anxious or asking for rescue. A differentiated leader is clear on her own values and convictions and is not easily swayed from them.

The opposites on either side of differentiation are enmeshment and detachment. An enmeshed leader is unable to hold any space between himself and the other. If the other is struggling, the enmeshed leader gets pulled into it. The detached leader holds too much space between himself and the other. There is so much space the leader does not care for the other. An enmeshed leader struggles with codependency but calls it empathy. The detached leader struggles with indifference and thinks it is healthy. In contrast, a differentiated leader is fully present, but fully intact, with space between where he or she ends and the other begins.

A differentiated leader offers nonanxious presence.

An enmeshed leader offers anxious presence.

A detached leader offers nonanxious absence.

Differentiation most powerfully comes into play when you lead a group of people where they do not want to go, but must go. Some of history's bravest leaders are often the most differentiated.

Marty Baron became editor of the *Boston Globe* newspaper, and on his first day, in his very first meeting where he was introduced to his staff, he dropped a bombshell on them. In his opinion, the *Boston Globe* had done very little to expose the systemic abuse of children at the hands of some Catholic priests, and he asked the reporters to dedicate significant resources to expose the cover-up. Almost all his staff were Catholic or former Catholics, and all were born and raised Boston citizens. Baron was a Jewish outsider, unconnected in Boston and a man of few words. The 2015 movie *Spotlight*, named after the investigative division of the *Globe*, details the Herculean effort of Baron and his reporters to uncover not only widespread sexual abuse but also the systemic, generational cover-up of the abuse.

In that first introductory meeting, several of Baron's new staff openly challenged Baron as an outsider and a critic of their work. But he remained differentiated. He was clear on his convictions and nonanxious in the face of their reactivity. Throughout the yearlong investigation several of Baron's team members also practiced differentiation as they had to confront old friends about their complicity in this sick system and even open threats from the archdiocese. Eventually, the *Globe* team even had to reckon with its own guilt at looking the other way all those years. Through this whole process, Baron and his team stayed connected—to one another, to the people of Boston, even to those threatening them with lawsuits and aggression if they continued their investigation.

The *Globe* eventually published more than six hundred articles detailing the abuse and the widespread cover-up; they also offered a hotline and help for abuse victims. In 2002 the *Globe* single-handedly turned the entire world's attention onto a global, multigenerational problem that affects us all. I recall the first time I watched the movie *Spotlight* and sat through the end credits where they showed every city in the world where the Catholic Church has covered up sexual abuse of minors. I have lived in several cities in my life, and every one of them was on the list. This seismic shift all started with a differentiated leader.

When Winston Churchill first became prime minister of England, the nation was on the brink of invasion. Germany had already taken Poland and Belgium and was actively occupying France. Churchill stepped into a politically volatile situation in England. He had a reputation for being hotheaded, a drunk, and a poor military leader. His disastrous tactic to fight Turkey on Gallipoli Beach during World War I was still hanging around his neck like a noose, and King George VI was a close friend of Churchill's top political rival.

Still, Germany was looming, England had three hundred thousand troops trapped in Dunkirk needing evacuation, and someone had to lead. The prevailing wisdom of Churchill's cabinet was to negotiate peace with Germany through the Italian prime minister Mussolini. Churchill's predecessor, Neville Chamberlain, had tried this and failed but still wanted to appease Hitler at any cost. But as Churchill so famously put it, "You can't negotiate with a tiger when your head is in its mouth." Churchill stood utterly alone politically, but was differentiated. He intentionally invited his political enemies and the former failed prime minister onto his war cabinet. He slowly won the respect of his king. He continued to lead where no one wanted to go: to fight to almost certain defeat rather than lay down in surrender. It is easy now to see that he knew what he was doing, but all objective data showed that his leadership would cause a massive death toll and certain occupation from Germany. He led the country to stand up to Hitler and they eventually won the war.

Churchill is a singular figure in history. Marty Baron and his team changed the world. Are these examples too unique, too big for the everyday leader? I use them because Baron and Churchill *are everyday leaders*. History has deemed them giants and their leadership wrought impactful change, but neither of them knew at the time that they were giants. They had no idea of the outcome of their leadership; they simply practiced stunning differentiation as they overcame resistance to bring true second-order change.

We naturally love stories where a person of conviction stands alone and changes the world, but standing alone is not differentiation. Differentiation is the courage to lead people to a difficult place while still being deeply connected. Connected to yourself and your conviction, connected to the people you are leading, and remaining nonanxious in the face of anxious responses. It is the ability to walk into an anxious situation and lead people into a new reality while maintaining caring connection to them even when they are sabotaging your efforts.

Jesus, not surprisingly, is a model of differentiated leadership. Consider Jesus on the road to Emmaus with Cleopas and his companion. Jesus walked alongside them in their struggle to make sense of all that was happening, but he did not carry them on his back. He was not, in fact, "carrying their burden," which an enmeshed person will be tempted to do. Nor did he feel any need to fix their problem by resolving who he was to them. Jesus was able to be connected to them in their grief without their anxiety infecting him. Thus they had a spiritual experience that they may not have had if Jesus had rushed in and said, "Guys, it's me! Jesus, the one you're talking about." Sometimes God has a growing opportunity for someone that an anxious leader shortchanges by trying to carry it for them. Jesus' capacity to walk alongside rather than carry, to listen rather than fix the folks on the way to Emmaus is stunning to me. Especially considering he was the very person they were grieving. But by waiting, "their eyes were opened" (Luke 24:31) and they experienced a deeper understanding. That is differentiated leadership. Leaders often grow anxious when someone is hurting or in need of an answer, but a differentiated person is able to manage that and be fully present to the person to see what God actually wants for him or her rather than shortchanging the person's own journey and growth in God.

Differentiation is the courage to lead people to a difficult place while still being deeply connected.

Becoming a differentiated leader is a journey, and none of us fully arrive. We are all continually on the spectrum of becoming more differentiated. A nonanxious leader is still often anxious, and still makes mistakes, raises his voice, or says regrettable things. Differentiation has nothing to do with being perfect or always calm. Differentiation is about managing your own anxiety and being aware of the contagious anxiety of a group while staying relationally connected to that group. None of us arrive at it, but we can all work toward it, so here are some early steps toward becoming differentiated.

- Using some of the earlier tools in this book, pay attention to your anxiety and work on reducing it before communicating with people. Communicating difficult topics without heat is a way to practice differentiation.
- Gain clarity on precisely what the problem and pattern is that you are facing. You may need to think, or even enlist some help, to map out the dynamic at play.
- Clarify your values and vision for what you are doing.
- Practice being exposed and vulnerable, even with a nonfriendly group.
- Clarify in your mind the difference between enmeshment and empathy. Clarify the difference between walking alongside people and carrying their burdens.

Scott Wyman has created a helpful diagram to show the spectrum of differentiation.[4]

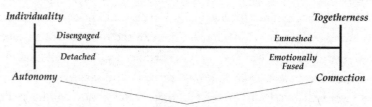

Individuality   *Togetherness*

  Disengaged   *Enmeshed*

  Detached   *Emotionally Fused*

Autonomy   *Connection*

Differentiation
is a process of:

*Discovering and celebrating
your "unique self"*

*And being that self,
without anxiety,
in relationship with another.*

Differentiation is a powerful tool, which means it can be co-opted by a toxic leader who thinks she is differentiated when she is not. You may be shuddering, having worked for a leader who stood alone, was wrong, and caused damage. If a leader isn't self-aware, or particularly if he is on the narcissism scale, then he might read this and decide he is a differentiated leader when actually he is simply alone. And that is how you know the difference. If you're not with these leaders, they are not differentiated. The dividing line of differentiation isn't agreement, it is relational connection and trust. Beware the narcissist, the ego-driven leader, or the person who is not self-aware: she can use these tools to cause more damage rather than more connection.

A final word about nonanxious presence. A nonanxious presence does not mean that you no longer battle anxiety, it means your anxiety no longer infects your system, and your capacity to manage others' anxiety is increased. Nonanxious presence was the goal of hospital chaplaincy, and it is the goal of every healthy leader. My capacity to be a nonanxious presence grew exponentially after I began to work on these principles in my first few weeks of chaplaincy. I could walk into a room, manage my own internal anxiety, and be differentiated in the face of overwhelming anxiety. I was fully present and empathetic. There was healthy space between me and the people I was serving, and because of that space I was able to serve them in their worst moments. Taking on their anxiety would not have served them, nor would being aloof to their pain. Keeping the space between us also awakened me to God who was there in the room offering peace into the storm. This was new for me. I had been a follower of God for a decade, but I had previously always rushed to fill that space with my own words or actions. In my own journey, I tend toward enmeshment over differentiation, but allowing this space to remain increased my awareness of God's Spirit and what God was up to.

Family systems theory is a decades-old field with hundreds of books. Of course, one chapter only scratches the surface of some very helpful family systems tools, so I have provided a bibliography at the end of this book for those who wish to explore further.

DISCUSSION QUESTIONS

1. Where have you seen health infect ill health?
2. Looking at process versus content, what process have you noticed in interactions? How can you increase your awareness of process while still paying attention to content?
3. Part of process is noticing when you are stuck. Can you think of a time when you have been stuck with someone?
4. Part of noticing process is paying attention to predictable, repeated patterns. Can you think of a pattern that you were in or someone you lead has been in? Can you map it out?
5. In the basketball story, the process was solved without ever dealing with content. (i.e., the boys never spoke about the issue at hand). How might you address a process issue with a process solution?
6. Problems are entrenched when we apply attempted solutions. Where have you seen this at work? How might you "prescribe the problem" back to break the stuck pattern?
7. How would you rate your differentiation? In what ways do you struggle with it?
8. On the spectrum of enmeshment to detachment, where do you fall?
9. What does empathy look like for a differentiated person? What is the difference between walking alongside and carrying another's burden?

seven

TOOLS THAT DIFFUSE ANXIETY

> *Anxiety, like sobriety, is best tackled one day and one step at a time. The important thing in either case is to not lose heart, and be kind to yourself.*
> —BRIAN W. FOSTER

Anxiety shrinks your world. It can encroach on you and show you a false reality that life is much worse than it really is. Anxiety's message: "There are only two options and they are both bad," or sometimes even "There are no good options." By using the tools discussed previously and in this chapter and by diffusing anxiety, you increase your capacity to see what is really true. These tools are designed to help you intervene early, de-escalate anxiety, and open up to the vistas of God that reside on the other side of self. Throughout the book I have offered some tools on the fly, so this chapter is somewhat of a catchall of what has not been previously covered. Most of these tools are quick to practice and much like the previous sources, some of these will resonate more naturally than others.

SELF TOOLS

Creating a Concrete, Life-giving List

One of the most common catalysts of anxiety is exhaustion. John Ortberg said, "Sometimes the most spiritual thing you can do is take a nap."[1] Colin Powell said, "Everything is better in the morning."[2] They are both saying the same basic principle: exhaustion clouds your thinking. Rest opens you back up to see clearly. But digging deeper, some exhaustion can't be addressed by sleep because the problem isn't simply rest, it is an imbalance of input and output. Too much doing for God, not enough abiding in God. It's a chronic problem most of us battle.

To put it more keenly, I struggle with the blurred line between being God's employee and God's child, that is, what I do for God and who I am in God. I clock in and work hard for the boss—the boss I love, for sure—but I can tend to cross-contaminate my identity in God with my work for God. This can lead to an input/output imbalance and also a creeping in of all gifts being used for church leadership, not for my own enjoyment.

Jesus assures us that God likes to give good gifts for his children. A few years ago, I realized that God had given me many gifts, not spiritual gifts to use for God's church but gifts from God for my own pleasure because I am his son. But I was not appreciating them. I changed that dynamic by making a written list of the gifts that God has given me for no other reason than I am his beloved son. Gifts I enjoy because they make me feel alive and human.

My list has three categories: people, places, and activities. They all have the same thing in common: they bring me life and energy that make me feel human and grateful. That's it. Nothing fancy, just a written list of who I enjoy, where I like to go, and what I enjoy doing that all ground me in being human, alive, and a child of God. I recommend you try this as well. Specifically, the list should be, "Gifts from God that remind me I am God's child, not an employee."

The list is best when it cannot benefit your vocation but causes you to feel more human, more alive, and more connected to God. The items on your list lead you to worship God and create a sense of deep gratitude and peace. They are life-giving people, places, and activities. We all have people who drain us, but hopefully also people who we simply enjoy. Write those names down. What about locations? Do you have any "thin places" where the distance between heaven and earth is thin—a pilgrimage location, or maybe a favorite mountain town or beach? What about activities? The list should have several options but should also factor in time. Some things on the list should be able to be done in minutes, others require a whole day or days.

My wife, for example, is on my people list. I have several people who bring me life, but at the top of the list are my wife and kids, whom I see as lavish gifts from God to me. I love anything in nature, so a drive to the mountains or the beach is always top of my list. For activities, I enjoy playing guitar, listening to music, fly fishing, rich conversation, wildlife, making good espresso, and reading theology. A day with my wife where we hike for a while, then I fish for a couple of hours while she reads a book under a tree, then we go out for dinner together afterward is literal heaven on earth for me. It is a multitude of gifts from God: my wife, nature, the beautiful trout, good food, rich conversation—all these are gifts God has given me that make me feel human. In case you're curious, no, I do not make my wife read under a tree so that I can be refreshed fishing. Reading under a tree by a stream happens to be on my wife's list. And yep, it is that specific.

One surprising activity on my list is spending two or three days at a local monastery doing a Gregorian chant of the Psalms with the local Benedictine nuns. I never thought that would make the list, but there is something about those simple chants with the nuns inside that rammed-earth chapel that really opens my soul to God.

Leaders in my tribe used to focus almost exclusively on Bible reading and prayer. We called it quiet time. That is on the list as well, but my list is a much broader set of connection tools that can be done in minutes, hours, and days. Sometimes just popping into the office of a friend or calling someone for a few minutes does it too. The list does not have to be elaborate or expensive, but it ought to be concrete and extensive. When I'm feeling dry and stretched thin, I pull out the list. It's amazing how the anxiety of ministry fades and the joy of being God's child comes in.

Some final words: if you don't put it on the calendar, it won't happen. I calendar some of these months in advance, like the two-day monastic retreat. Sometimes I rearrange my week to allow more input. Sometimes a significant crisis pops up that I have to deal with, but it drains me, so I add an appointment to my week of something from my list. Once it's on my calendar, it is sacrosanct. People want my time and I simply answer, "Sorry, I already have an appointment." That appointment may well be with a trout or a guitar or my wife, not necessarily in that order.

Capacity to Care for People

Another simple tool of anxiety reduction is to consider your capacity to care for people. We all have to wrestle with the tension of when to pour yourself out for someone and when to fill yourself up and serve out of the overflow. How do you know when your serving capacity is full?

Depending on personality and wiring, some people serve by emptying themselves. If you are one of these people, it takes very little for you to immediately drop what you are doing if another person is in need. You give all for the cause, whatever it takes; you die on any hill. You take great pride in being there for people, going the extra mile, sacrificing yourself. You are someone who pours yourself out, but have you ever considered your overall capacity, or do you naturally think, *Just one more, I can do it?* That mind-set has you in sight of burning out, having nothing left to give. You may even find yourself feeling alone at times, wondering why people don't seem to care that you give so much.

When is God calling you to pour it all out, and when is God calling you to fill yourself first and serve out of the overflow?

Others are wired differently. They naturally hold back, conserving energy. These folks are happy to help but are not the first to step in, or they have no problem saying, "I am already helping these people. My plate is full."

One type of person believes he or she has unending energy and capacity to pour into someone; the other believes that he or she must wisely conserve energy for when it really counts. You can typically figure out which way you're wired by your reaction to the opposite. Neither are wrong. Both can very much fulfill Jesus' command to love your neighbor as yourself. The question is, When is God calling you to pour it all out, and when is God calling you to fill yourself first and serve out of the overflow?

I tend toward the first dynamic. It is difficult for me to admit that I am at capacity, and I tend to pour out, out, out, ignoring the Refill Soon sign on my dashboard. Until I really paused to think about it, I assumed I had an unending tank. Those who are more cautious may have more gallons in your tank than you naturally think. Knowing and recognizing capacity, and especially knowing when to fill up your own tank before pouring out to others, is key to ongoing soul health.

Workload Scrub

The most effective leaders I know have a "whatever it takes" approach that means they find themselves doing tasks and projects they do not need to be giving time toward. Over time, we can find ourselves anxious by the sheer scope of work we have on our plates. One simple way to rightsize this is to do a workload scrub. The first time could be painful but it is generally liberating.

Open a spreadsheet with four columns. In the first column write every single thing you do for your organization during the course of a year. My list typically has around 120 items on it. The next column shows an estimate of the hours per month each task takes. The final column is a simple yes or no question: Can someone else do this task or project? The fourth column is the name of the person.

For the first eight years of my time at our church, I shot and edited videos for testimonies. I am not naturally gifted at video production, but I took a class, read a lot, and did my best. Any video story was better than no video story, right? Those who are experienced in video production can attest to how many hours a single project can take. Our church also leased a large format banner printer for a while and I was the only staff member who could consistently get it to work. Anytime someone needed to print, I ended up getting involved.

We all take on projects or tasks that we have no business doing, and the particularly insidious tasks are the "I'll do this one time" tasks that end up on your plate more permanently. Creating a workload scrub takes a few hours; it is not a simple endeavor. My key leaders do one annually as do I, and I am always amazed at what has ended up on my plate that ought not be there.

If you are battling anxiety, it could simply be because your work has become too broad in scope and too deep in projects. For a few years our church didn't show video testimonies because I scrubbed them off my list. The day we handed the banner printer back to the leasing company, I went out for sushi to celebrate.

What are you doing that is way outside your scope and role? How many hours are you putting in and what should get scrubbed off your list? A quick final note: a poor leader will write names on the scrub list and simply task those items to someone else. A healthy leader will see what he or she needs to stop doing and build a team, outsource, or give a team member appropriate ramp-up time to take on the role.

Listening to Learn Versus Listening to Defend

The title of this one is also the explanation. My wife is a therapist who recently completed graduate school. One day she came home from a class with this powerful nugget, and as soon as she said it, I was skewered by it. I do too much listening to defend and not enough listening to learn. I am a driven type A leader who likes to convince and inspire. Among my peers I am naturally more wired to defend and convince than I am to listen and understand. Ouch. I now walk into an anxious meeting having already decided to work on listening to learn rather than defend. You can diffuse a lot of anxiety, in the other person and in yourself, if you commit to listen to learn.

My friend Kim Skattum once told our staff, "So often when people tell you their problems, you feel ill-equipped to help them, like what they really need is a social worker or a counselor. But people aren't telling you their problem expecting you to become a professional. They just want you to understand. Listen at least until you see by their demeanor that they feel understood." I thought that was great, tangible advice.

The Gift of the Last Word

The gift of the last word is closely related to the tool immediately above. Oh, how I want to be right and how I want to be understood. They are twin idols in my life that I need, I need, I need; and when I don't get either, I get very anxious. If someone misunderstands what I am saying, particularly when he or she misattributes my motives, I get anxious. The gift of the last word is a simple, sometimes painful technique to overcome these needs. Someone must have the last word. It no longer must be me. I will be okay without the last word, which means I am okay being misunderstood. I reject the fallacy that one more response from me is what we need to move on. You get the final say. I will sit here being misunderstood, and it is okay.

Recovering from Mistakes

In chapter 3 we looked at how mistakes can generate much anxiety for a leader, but recovering from them can diffuse it. Leaders want to understate their mistakes, but if you understate them you'll never experience the grace of forgiveness and unconditional love that God offers. Why not instead rightsize them? Look your mistakes right in the eye, repent of them, learn from them, and forgive yourself. God forgave you long ago.

Once in a while, one of my staff will make a whopper leadership mistake, and I'll ask him to write out everything he did wrong in the mistake. I am not rubbing his nose in it. Instead, I'm offering him an experience of grace. He gets to hold his mistakes in his hands without shame. He also sees the implication of the mistake and the damage it caused, and then he gets to forgive himself and open himself up to the grace of God who so freely forgives. Fortunately for our staff, their lead pastor is chief mistake maker in residence. And I'm not shy about sharing my mistakes. They aren't pretty mistakes, and some are even cringeworthy. The worst ones are the ones I make when I should know better. But when you move into your mistake rather than skimming the surface, you actually relax because you no longer have to hide and blame (the two chief tools of responding to a mistake). Once you've written the list, looked at it, and repented of it, you can be vulnerable again and will rarely make the same mistake twice. The Catholic Church has the wonderful, tangible tool of confession, but we Protestants don't practice confession and so can tend to hold on to our mistakes with a low-level shame for years. Better to look the mistake in the eye and move on.

RELATIONAL TOOLS

Name the Dynamic

When people come to me and ask how they should handle anxiety between them and another person, they often do a beautiful job of succinctly laying out the exact dynamic. After explaining the situation and the dynamic, they ask what to do. My most frequent response is, "Can you tell them exactly what you just told me?" When you are stuck in a pattern with someone, the very best way to diffuse anxiety is to name that pattern with the person.

"Hey, I've noticed that you ask for help, and when I try to help, you get quite frustrated. Can you help me understand what is going on there, because I want to help, but I feel like I'm in trouble with you when I do. I feel in a double bind."

"Oh, sorry about that. By the time I ask for help, I'm already mad at myself for not knowing how to do it. I don't mean for that to bleed over to you. I just feel like an idiot when I can't figure this out."

The absolute secret to this conversation going well is your ability to have it without heat. If you are angry at someone, or really wound up and anxious, take time to remove the heat from the situation before addressing it with him or her. Talking about a dynamic between you is vulnerable and could be threatening, especially for an indirect communicator. It could escalate or de-escalate the dynamic and anxiety, and the magic secret is removing heat and anxiety when you talk.

Repair Work

Repair work is one of the simplest but most difficult tools to diffuse anxiety. We all create a mess once in a while. We all say things we did not mean, lose our cool, or treat someone in a way we regret. But few people know how to go back and repair the damage; instead they avoid it or minimize it, but those attempted solutions only make it worse. Why not repair it instead? If you know someone you did not treat well, you can simply approach that person and give him or her some context and an apology.

Say something like, "Here is what I did and I regret how I did it. Here is where I was coming from. I am not saying that to excuse it. I know it caused damage, and I am sorry for the hurt that it caused. I would like to hear how it affected you." Repair work takes humility and courage, but also builds significant trust and relational equity. The simplest repair is when you acknowledge what you did, apologize for it, and acknowledge the impact it had on the other. An apology without an acknowledgment of impact isn't enough. But most people will give each other grace for these situations if repair is handled well.

Recognize Who Is Moving Toward You and Who Is Not

How much energy have you expended trying to lead people who are not remotely interested in your leadership? You try all kinds of tricks, but at the end of the day the people won't follow you. One of the reasons they may not be following you is because of how much you want them to. Some people are just born contrary; others need time to trust, and the more you convince the less they trust. Sometimes it is you, sometimes it is the other person, but most often it is the dynamic between you. Here is a universal truth: you can only lead people who are moving toward you.

You can only lead people who are moving toward you.

If someone isn't moving toward you, you can coerce that person, maybe. You may even get him or her to do something, but you won't have that person's trust. You cannot lead someone in a healthy way if he or she does not trust you, and you cannot lead someone who is moving away from you. Leadership becomes how to appropriately get people to move toward you and how to steward the people who are already moving toward you. Healthy leadership also recognizes when people are no longer moving toward you.

Jesus, of course, was the maestro at this. He seemingly allowed people to come and go without ever chasing them. There is no way, for example, that I would have let the rich young ruler walk. My tendency is to pursue people who are moving away from me. Jesus, in contrast, stood his ground and watched as people turned and left (Mark 10:17–27).

If you are battling anxiety about how one member of your team keeps showing up, you can pause and reflect on if he or she is postured toward you. George Bernard Shaw said, "The single biggest problem with communication is the illusion that it has taken place." If the person to whom you are communicating is not facing you, you are not communicating with them.

Edwin Friedman wrote, "The colossal misunderstanding of our time is that more insight will work with people who are unmotivated to change. Communication does not depend on syntax, or eloquence, or rhetoric, or articulation but on the emotional context in which the message is being heard. *People can only hear you when they are moving toward you*" (emphasis added).[3]

Reframing

Anxiety is caused by thinking things are bigger than they really are. Oftentimes people describe their feelings using superlatives and exaggeration, and by doing so they shrink their future down to a fatalistic outlook. It is often easiest to spot in children because children are wired to think in absolutes and superlatives.

If you hear someone say, "You always" or, "I never," you can receive that and reframe it for him or her. Reframing is the ability to notice these absolutes and superlatives and to offer a gentle rearranging of this assumption. Reframing rightsizes someone's anxiety by inviting the person to see the same situation in a more nuanced, more accurate way. Reframing is a difficult balance because it can feel like manipulation, but the best reframing is offered to someone out of care. It doesn't dismiss his or her fear; it just more accurately captures the situation.

Let's say someone remarks, "James always treats me like I'm an idiot."

A way to reframe in a caring way might be to say, "So you're saying that when James sometimes speaks to you, he is condescending and that feels belittling to you?"

If your reframe is inaccurate, you can count on the person telling you. But more often than not, people get locked into absolutes and superlatives, which escalate and exaggerate anxiety. Learning to listen for these triggers and offering a gentle reframe can be a gift to the person who is anxious because it helps him or her rightsize the situation.

God, it turns out, is quite the reframer.

In 1 Kings 19:14 Elijah told God, "I have been very zealous for the LORD God Almighty. The Israelites have rejected your covenant, torn down your altars, and put your prophets to death with the sword. I am the only one left, and now they are trying to kill me too." Was this accurate? Had *all* the Israelites rejected God's covenant, or just a great many of them? Was Elijah the *only* one left? *All* and *only one* are trigger words that show we could have cared for Elijah by reframing reality for him. The good news of God is better than the bad news of doom and isolation that Elijah was seeing. Reality was in better shape than he believed.

Just a couple of verses later God replied, "Anoint Jehu son of Nimshi king over Israel, and anoint Elisha son of Shaphat from Abel Meholah to succeed you as prophet. . . . I reserve seven thousand in Israel—all whose knees have not bowed down to Baal and whose mouths have not kissed him" (vv. 16, 18). God was reframing reality for Elijah. All of Israel had not rejected God but quite the opposite. There were at least two whom God saw fit to anoint as chosen to serve in a particular way. Further, there were at least seven thousand faithful people who, like Elijah, had rejected Baal.

You'll be surprised at how often you also could use some reframing.

The initial signal that someone needs a reframe are superlatives and exaggeration, but another type of person who can be reframed is the always intense or the always discouraged person. Have you ever worked with a leader who only ever offered a strong opinion and for whom everything was always urgent? You can even reframe someone like that: "You are someone who feels strongly about a lot of things and you come across as if everything is urgent. On the overall scale of urgency, how urgent is this?"

Or: "When you communicate strongly about every initiative, you lose authority with your team because they have to scale in their own minds what is most important and what is less important. You will become a more powerful leader if you can manage that scale yourself and learn to communicate with a greater range of intensity. When everything is important, nothing is important."

This is a delicate balance, particularly if your reframing sends the unintended message, "You're blowing it out of proportion." That is not a reframe. Appropriate reframing should bring relief to someone, not make him or her feel misunderstood. Skilled reframing is an act of kindness when it rightsizes people's anxiety and when it serves a group who may not know how to handle a strong personality.

Some personalities *need* to feel alone like Elijah did. It is part of their identity and worth. "I stand alone and no one in the world stands with me." It is never true, of course, as Elijah learned, but if you find people fighting you when you reframe, they may have an idol of needing to be alone so the stories they tell themselves stay intact. You'll need to proceed gently and patiently with people like that until they can see the better news that they are less alone than they want to be.

Take the Problem As Seriously or More Seriously Than the Person

This can appear to be in opposition to the reframing technique above, but it's actually a different tool. When people come and share their struggles with you, you can sometimes catch their anxiety and become overwhelmed by what they are telling you. You are then possibly tempted to "lighten" the anxiety by sending them some form of the message, "It's not that bad." But if instead you take their problem as seriously or more seriously than they do, it communicates, "I care, I hear you, I comprehend the depth of what you're going through," and inexplicably, it also reduces your anxiety because it rightsizes the situation.

You may be thinking, *Didn't you just instruct us to reframe someone, now you're telling us to make it worse?* Reframing is for exaggeration and superlatives, for people who are always intense and urgent, people who are describing their situations in unrealistic terms. Taking the problem as seriously as the person is a technique to keep you from shrinking the problem because of your own anxiety response.

When we don't know what to do in the face of high emotion or real trauma, we can do damage by giving in to our internal pressure to make it better. Taking the situation as seriously or more seriously communicates "I hear you, I understand you," but it also quiets your own internal desire to move out of the high emotion. If someone is sharing something that you truly are not equipped to help with, the kind move is to simply tell him or her. I frequently tell people, "This one is over my skill level. I'm glad you reached out for help because this really is a significant problem, but I am going to help by finding someone who can help you better than me, and I won't let you go until you're in that person's hands."

So, reframing is reducing anxiety by rightsizing exaggeration. Taking the problem at least as seriously is the other side of the same coin—still rightsizing, but this time it is rightsizing your impulse to reduce the size of the problem. It is the opposite of "It's not that bad" and "Look on the bright side."

If you are trying to listen to someone and are missing what he is saying or he is speaking in such overwhelming ways that you cannot clarify their intent, you can try *doubling*, a therapy technique available to leaders. It started in Greek theater where a stage actor would say a line and then the chorus would double the line by rephrasing it.

Perhaps someone is either overwhelmed and incoherent in her communication or she struggles to put words to what she is thinking and feeling. You can say, "I'd like to double you. I will say what I think you are saying because I want to make sure I am understanding. After that, either say 'Yes, that's it' or correct me." It is a simple but empathic form of caring for someone and getting clarity on what is the issue at hand.

If you're wrong and she corrects you, it helps her clarify by listening to what you think she is saying, and it helps you clarify as you listen to her correction. If you nailed it, it says to her, "This person understands." Doubling can be very helpful for people who are so anxious that they are struggling to communicate in the moment. You can double them and help them catch their breath and "hear their brain" through your voice.

Intentionally Move Toward the Person You Are Struggling With

There is something very dark in us that becomes self-righteous when we're anxious or hurt by someone. It plays out most keenly in the story we tell ourselves about a person with whom we are in conflict. By the time we are done with an anger fantasy, the person is subhuman. We have stripped him or her of nuance and dimension and made the person worse than he or she really is. This dynamic also happens in gossip, triangulation, and judgment.

The solution to de-escalate anxiety happens to line up with the gospel: move toward the person. I wonder if this is partly why Jesus commanded us to love our enemy. Jesus commanded it because we don't want to do it. We want to stay removed, gossip about the person to others, build a case against her in our minds. But all that leads to more anxiety. Could it be that Jesus commanded us to love our enemy because he knows that proximity is what helps you see more of someone's humanity and more of her image bearing?

If you find someone's comment or behavior has made you anxious, make the move closer to him. Some people are along the narcissism scale or even pathological, so proceed with caution with those folks as they will simply use your goodwill against you again and again. But for most people, proximity reduces anxiety.

Managing the Energy in the Room

What would your meetings be like if you paid as much attention to people's energy as you did to the agenda? Much like our previous focus on process as well as content, a skilled leader learns to run a meeting based on energy levels, not just the task at hand. You can de-escalate anxiety and increase participation by structuring your agenda to inject energy into the meeting at strategic times.

Before our elder meetings, our chair, vice chair, and I meet to plan the agenda, and we spend as much time on energy management as we do on content. We intentionally order the content in a way that keeps people most engaged and most enjoying the time.

Our staff meetings are the same. Energy is not difficult to create. Laughter creates energy, as does a good story, discussion, breaking into groups, physically moving around, clapping, and giving out awards or prizes. Our meetings have developed a tradition of goofy prizes: sometimes we give out a free ream of paper autographed by one of our staff members or a gift card to a restaurant. Other times our prizes have themes, like the time we gave out items from the produce aisle of our supermarket. We literally handed out romaine lettuce, an avocado, and a carrot as prizes. Prizes give the double bonus of laughter and honoring someone for their good work.

We also get people out of their chairs, move from monologue to discussion, and break into smaller groups. Anything to manage the energy of a meeting. You can set an agenda and then map the agenda like an EKG graph and try to keep the participation high. And this leads us to our next tool.

The Importance of Not Being Earnest

One of the simplest ways to de-escalate anxiety is to develop a knack for playfulness. Ed Friedman says, "A major criterion for judging the anxiety level of any society is the loss of its capacity to be playful."[4] Playfulness is a form of reframing without having to reframe directly. You can simply bring some levity into the situation. You'll know the playfulness worked if the group relaxes, and didn't work if the group looks at you sideways because your attempt was ill-timed or in poor taste. Yes, I've experienced both.

A few tips: playfulness works best when not directly aimed at the issue or person at hand. You should not try to seek a laugh at the expense of the matter at hand or the person in question. Playfulness should be equally enjoyed by all, and so the best playfulness offers a relief valve for the building pressure of anxiety or the exhaustion of a long meeting focused on an important, detailed task.

Absurdity is a safe form of playfulness. The example with Mr. Quiet, who didn't speak up in meetings, had a significant amount of absurdity built in, which kept his anxiety lowered because of the fun built into his solution. Optimism is also a form of playfulness. Colin Powell said, "Optimism is a force multiplier," and a leader should recognize the simple power of optimism to work toward a better future.

One form of playfulness is the simple but serious question, "What is the worst that could happen?" One of our team frequently replies, "I don't think anyone will die from this," which usually rightsizes the task at hand over which we have all become too earnest. Earnestness is the opposite of playfulness, so people who take themselves too seriously and are unable to laugh at themselves could often use a dose of playfulness.

One of the ways you'll know your team needs some playfulness is by paying attention to the energy in the room. Playfulness can also serve an additional benefit of opening up possibilities when things seem bleak. We are getting pretty nuanced here: reframing, taking the problem seriously, and playfulness can all appear at odds with one another. But they are different tools for different occasions, and you'll only sort it out by trying, and therefore getting it wrong from time to time. Having said that, a mistimed effort at playfulness that fails can itself become a source of de-escalation if your group has a high level of trust with one another.

The tools in the following chapters go deeper into some significant ways to lower anxiety, but the tools discussed in this chapter are simple, quick, and, with practice, can be added to a leader's tool belt. The success of these tools is dependent on your capacity for vulnerability and courage. All of them involve putting yourself out there, possibly failing, and moving forward in the face of fear and anxiety.

DISCUSSION QUESTIONS

1. How do you know when you are exhausted? When do you know it is physical and mental exhaustion, and when do you know it is spiritual emptiness?

2. What might be on your list of people, places, and activities?

3. How difficult is it for you to offer someone the gift of the last word? Why is it so difficult? Does having the last word accomplish what you want?

4. Have you ever tried to lead someone who is not moving toward you? What was it like? What did you do? What would you do different knowing that person is not moving toward you? What would it take for you to trust him or her to someone else rather than try to win that person over?

5. Have you ever tried reframing or needed reframing yourself? What about taking a problem as seriously as the person sharing? What is the difference and how do you know which tool to use when?

6. Have you ever tried to move closer to someone you're struggling with? What was it like? If not, does someone come to mind? How about someone dangerous like a narcissist or highly toxic person? How is that different?

7. Do you know anyone who is good at being appropriately playful? How about mistimed and ill-judged playfulness?

8. Which tools are you going to try this week?

eight

GENOGRAMS: WHAT HAS
BEEN HANDED DOWN

*Our identities are formed through the
sphere of those who matter to us most.*
—ERWIN MCMANUS

Previous chapters moved quickly through several tools that help manage anxiety, but these next two chapters slow down to focus on one significant tool each. Counselors use a genogram, the first deep tool, to help individuals and couples understand how their families of origin impact their relationships, but leaders can also do a genogram. It will take a few hours of preparation and then another hour or so to present to your peers, but the effort is worth it. I have helped dozens of people through their genograms, and without fail, leaders come away with fresh perspective on who they are and why they show up the way they do. A genogram helps you see the cards you have been dealt, what you are holding onto, and what is holding onto you.

This material will invite you to explore what could be painful memories, and I want to caution anyone who has come out of an abusive background that some of this material may trigger some powerful memories or even cause damage. If you experience PTSD or have survived significant trauma in your life, this material might best be explored with a trusted therapist who is trained to create a safe environment for trauma. This tool is not an occasion for blame, but for deeper insight into your worldview and triggers.

And so, the genogram.

I think it must be very difficult to find your place in a family with a celebrity in it. Everybody wants to talk about your actress mother or your politician grandfather who ran for president. You endure six or seven questions about your famous relative until the person finally asks, "What about you? What do you do?" Your most honest response is, "Not much." That was Jason. He endured being related to two very famous people. Everybody in the world, literally, knew his grandfather, and many knew his less famous but iconic younger brother, Sheridan. People only knew of Jason in relation to them, not for who he was. People looked through Jason to see his celebrity family or sometimes befriended him to get to them. He was looked over and looked past.

Jason was a solidly built guy, son of a farmer, a salt of the earth type. He didn't speak much, and while he had a good brain, he did not have a quick brain, and certainly not a witty one like his brother nor a wise one like his grandfather. Jason was nothing more or less than normal, which is to say he was invisible. He didn't think fast, but he felt deep, and what he felt most was anger, like the world owed him something. He didn't battle entitlement like some people born into wealth, but a general underlying feeling that he was being taken advantage of because of his good nature. Jason's deep-seated anger made sense when you study his genogram.

A genogram is a family tree sketched out on butcher paper, or sometimes digitally using an app. On it, you record names and births and deaths like a family tree, then add extra information like divorces, remarriage, affairs, miscarriages, mental health. You also record relational health using various diagrams—who got along with whom, who was in tension, who was cut off, who was a favorite, who was a secret keeper. Once you've sketched out your genogram, including all the relational keys and major events, you gather some trusted friends and present your family history for an hour or so.

At the end of this chapter, I've provided guiding questions your friends can ask to help you see recurring patterns and generational traits of your family. You'll also learn assumptions that you always thought were true but may not be. A genogram helps you see the traits passed down from generation to generation. While a genogram may reveal some significant challenge from your upbringing, it is not about blame or being a victim. A genogram is about understanding what you're holding and what is holding you in your family system. As Seth Godin wrote, "It's not your fault, but it might be your responsibility. That's a fork in the road on the way to becoming a professional."[1]

Jason had experienced two monumental events by the time he'd reached adulthood, one he was too young to remember and one he would never forget. Both events had profound impact on his worldview. Jason was the oldest of twins, and his younger brother was the celebrity. When they were born, his younger brother had him by the heel as Jason came out of the womb. Jason was literally helping his brother be born by going first, but that's not how the rest of the world understood it—others interpreted it as Sheridan striving to get ahead while his dimwitted brother did nothing about it.

A genogram is about understanding what you're holding and what is holding you in your family system.

Jason's childhood was filled with his own mother blatantly favoring his brother every chance she could. His dad never intervened. He just sat by unengaged. From Jason's earliest memories, he had to stand up for himself, but he always lost when pitted against a quick-witted brother and a colluding mother. He loved his younger brother and felt a sense of protection for him, but his brother didn't return the feeling. And as much as Jason didn't like to admit it, Sheridan was smarter and cunning; he knew how to manipulate an advantage.

Jason's birth was the first event. The second event sealed it. Sheridan literally tricked his dad into signing over Jason's inheritance, and by the time Jason got wind of it, the papers had been filed and the inheritance moved.

As you may have guessed by now, Jason is Esau and Sheridan is Jacob from the Old Testament book of Genesis. Jacob's grandfather was Abraham, the literal father of all nations, one of the top five most famous people in history.

No matter what you think of Esau, we can all agree that he was dealt a rough hand when he was born. And yes, I named his brother Sheridan because I'm pretty sure if Jacob were alive today, he'd be touring in a boy band. Esau's brother fought him for birth order status, and his mother favored his scoundrel brother at every turn, even colluding with him in the inheritance scam. His father was completely uninvolved because his own worldview was deeply impacted by a near-death experience at a formative age, at the hand of his father, Abraham.

Esau would have benefitted from looking at his genogram because it would have allowed him to see some generational patterns in his family. One generational trait was deceit. Jacob was a third-generation deceiver, and generational deceit impacted each member in the family. Some family members colluded in the deceit, some were victims of it. If we focused on Jacob's genogram instead of Esau's, we'd see how deceit impacted his spiritual outlook. Jacob saw everyone in the world, including God, as someone he had to work over. If we were participating in Jacob's genogram, we might ask him to consider why he always believed he had to be someone else in order to be blessed. Jacob began to grow when he realized he could be blessed by God because of grace, not because of his own huckstering. "I will not let you go unless you bless me," Jacob once said to God while wrestling him (32:26). Blessing on his terms and conditions. But that is not how blessing works.

A genogram gives insight into what you value, where your resilience comes from, and why you see the world the way you do. It invites you to sift your assumptions through the truth of Scripture.

In my own life, I have a mother who is incredibly witty, skilled at anything she puts her hand to, is never a bother to anyone, and will do anything for anyone. I am very proud to be her son, and I have inherited many positive traits from her. But one of the traits I have had to wrestle with is the general self-sufficiency in our family. Someone who will do anything for anyone often will not ask for help or even think her problems are worthy of another's help. Presenting my genogram when I was in my twenties was eye-opening to the impact this had on my worldview. My genogram group showed me that the family propaganda I was presenting to them was, "Other people have real problems; other people have it harder than us. I don't have any problems that need significant help." They invited me to consider the very real and impactful struggles I have and how I was dysfunctionally covering them up with my behaviors. This family worldview, a strength in many ways, had a shadow side that impacted my connection to God.

I have a lifelong struggle to experience God's love for me particularly; my default position is to experience it generically, like I am number 24601 generic human who is generically loved by God, rather than Steve, beloved son of God. Part of the obstacle is my family propaganda that "others have it worse." Cusses are needed, not needy. Needy is vulnerable, and vulnerable is the only way to open my heart to God's very particular and specific love for me. I would not have seen this so starkly if not for my genogram. I have found freedom in believing the good news, which in this particular case means believing what Jesus and Paul revealed about God's love over what I believe is true about God's love. Faith, for me, is trusting Jesus and Paul more than I trust myself and my family propaganda.

I'll say it again: a genogram has no interest in blame, it's only interested is showing you the hand you've been dealt. You can play it more effectively if you know what you're holding and what is holding onto you. What are you gripping? What has you in its grip? A genogram can help clarify that.

Exodus contains a startling promise, "The LORD, the LORD, the compassionate and gracious God, slow to anger, abounding in love and faithfulness, maintaining love to thousands, and forgiving wickedness, rebellion and sin. Yet he does not leave the guilty unpunished; he punishes the children and their children for the sin of the parents to the third and fourth generation" (34:6–7).

I'll confess this is a puzzling promise. On the one hand, God is compassionate and gracious; on the other hand, he punishes guilty people by making their grandchildren and great grandchildren pay for their sins. This "promise" is not exactly exciting news, certainly not good news at first blush, but I think it is. God forgives, yet the guilty continue to transmit the impact of their guilt down through the generations. While I'm sure the author of this passage didn't have this in mind, the principle is the same: those who are not aware of what they are gripping and what has a grip on them are doomed to pass it down generation to generation. Those who do not seek forgiveness and develop awareness of their habits and traits are doomed to pass their guilt down through their family system, even to their great grandchildren. From a family systems perspective, the promise from Exodus is, "If you come to God, God stops you from staining your family tree. If you don't your stain will carry down through the generations."

This generational transmission is not always negative of course.

Our families also transmit positive, healthy traits through the generations. In my family, for example, I have inherited a wonderful sense of
adventure. I spent my early years at the race track and then scrambling
on rocks while my parents fished, watching for waves that could wash
us off. Most of my hobbies and interests are directly related to my mum
and dad's interests and even my grandparent's interests, and I'm proud
of that.

Even looking at painful transmission can be freeing. For example,
I have known people who battle mental illness. Some forms of mental illness are incredibly isolating and shaming. Not only is a person
fighting the technical illness, he or she bravely fights the extra baggage
that comes with it: shame and isolation. I've seen people experience
freedom when they discover that their mental illness is hereditary. It
is not their fault. They feel less shame and blame and realize that it is
something handed down to them, or often they realize, "I am not as
alone as I thought I was." Often, in a genogram, an ancestor or older
family member won't be diagnosed. The presenter may say something
like, "This was before we really understood mental illness, but looking back at Aunt Mary and what she did, I think she might have had
bipolar disorder."

The promise of Exodus is a double-edged sword for sure, but having the courage to see what you are holding and what is holding you
can free you from passing on traits you don't want to pass on. You may
say, "Wait just a hot minute. If some traits are hereditary, how I can
I stop them from being passed down?" You can't stop the hereditary
traits, but you can powerfully break all that comes with them—the
secrecy, shame, and baggage.

The author of Exodus wrote like it was a promise, but I think he
was simply defining reality: without the power of God, we all pass our
sins down to the third and fourth generation. Even if we are aware
of traits and try to deal with them on our own, we can't break their
generational power. It is simply what happens in all families, but God

has the power to break generational sin. I think this is what Jeremiah was getting at when he wrote:

> In those days people will no longer say, "The parents have eaten sour grapes, and the children's teeth are set on edge." Instead, everyone will die for their own sin; whoever eats sour grapes—their own teeth will be set on edge. (Jer. 31:29–30)

Without a family systems point of view, this doesn't sound much like good news, but it really is. Jeremiah was also defining reality. It was actually good news. Jeremiah was saying that a day will come when the gospel of God will intercede into generational traits and stop the sins of the father being visited upon the children.

Making and presenting a genogram is a deeper level of work. Constructing it takes at least two or three hours, longer if you need to get on the phone with a relative. Sometimes those phone calls generate more work too! Once you've constructed a genogram, you'll spend another hour to ninety minutes presenting it to a group of friends. But the time is worth it. We grow in fits, starts, and breakthroughs, and a genogram can offer you some powerful breakthroughs. I learned a great deal when I first presented a genogram more than twenty years ago. The beauty of presenting a genogram to a group is that both the presenter and the group learn something about themselves.

Four recurring themes to look for in a genogram are: *cutoff, enmeshment, conflict*, and *abuse*. We commonly understand conflict and abuse, and we have covered enmeshment in our discussion on differentiation, so we will spend the rest of this chapter diving deeper into cutoff.

If dysfunction is not named and addressed, it is transmitted down to the next generation, which will commonly deal with it through cutoff. Cutoff often comes in the form of a childhood vow, "When I am an adult, I will never _____ like my parent did."

A few years ago, James presented a genogram and learned some insight about himself and his family trait. He said, "There has not been a generation on either side of my family that hadn't cut off significantly sideways and up the tree. Our family has sibling cutoff and parent cutoff in several generations." James was an only child and grew up with no connection or interactions with his cousins, aunts, or uncles. He started to realize how unusual this was when he would visit friends' homes. He would notice that his friends would have thirty family members over for Christmas, or they would go on a vacation to see extended family, but he only spent time with his mum and dad.

In James's family, cutoff was connected to bad business deals and to religion. His great grandparents and his grandfather cut off over business deals. His father and grandfather cut off over religious leadership. James grew up irreligious, but had a profound encounter with Jesus as a teenager and not only became a follower of Christ but wanted to become a pastor. So, when he told his dad, "I am going to be a pastor," his father responded, "Then you're not my son," and cut him off.

Of course, at the time, James interpreted this cutoff through a Christian martyrdom lens: "I am suffering for Christ." That was true, but it was not all the truth in the situation. What is also true is what James learned years later when he did some genogram work. His father's grandfather was a Brahmin Indian who took a Hindu vow of poverty. His

Cutoff is a process of separation, isolation, withdrawal, running away or denying the importance of the parental family.[2]

religious devotion had a negative impact on his family, who then cut him off and lived under the assumption that "religion cuts people off and negatively impacts people." This was true in that particular instance, but as we've seen, we become bound when we take an instance of truth and make it universally true. James's grandfather did actual damage when he became a religious leader. True. But that truth became a binding universal in his family: "All religious leaders cause damage."

When James, an only child, said to his father, "I want to become

a pastor," his father heard, "I want to damage the family." From his
dad's point of view, he wasn't persecuting his son for his faith, he was
trying to protect his family. This insight doesn't reduce the pain and
impact, it just widens our understanding of the dynamic, because
when you inhabit someone else's story, his decision often makes
more sense to you and dissolves cognitive dissonance and anxiety. By
understanding his dad's perspective, James was both freed from the
sting of rejection and also able to stay connected to a father who was
actively trying to disconnect from him.

James poignantly told me, "Jesus cut off the cutoff. Jesus rebuilds
the bridge that humans cut off." James sensed God telling him, *You
have to forgive your dad and bless him. You don't have to wait for him to
behave the right way, you can no longer use his behavior as justification.*

A fascinating aside in this story: James received encouragement
and even reinforcement from his church community in the early
days of his cutoff from his father. Churchgoers translated his dad's
behavior as a form of persecution and thus James was a martyr for
the cause. Didn't Jesus himself make extreme statements about faithfulness to God and walking away from your parents? While it is
technically true that James's dad *was* exhibiting a form of persecution, that was far from the whole story. By encouraging James, the
church was causing more damage, giving James a shrunken truth.
James sought to pray for his dad and forgive his dad, and the church
leaders were unintentionally rewarding cutoff by telling James, "You
are the bigger man."

But to James's great credit, he chose to look at the ways he was
contributing to the dysfunction, and he spent a decade reversing the
cutoff habit. That is because James knows the truth of the gospel that
we discussed in chapter 6: health infects ill health. Without the gospel, emotional disease causes infection. With the gospel, emotional
health is the infecting agent. Emotional health can slowly "infect"
emotional disease and make it better.

It took James and his parents seventeen years of slow progress, sometimes experiencing regression, sometimes experiencing breakthrough. It was slow, messy, and painful. One of my great fears in writing this book is that I will give the false impression that this work is quick, easy, or comes with a guaranteed outcome. Family patterns take years, even decades, to reverse, not weeks.

James's early bumbling attempts to stay connected paid off as he learned more family systems theory and how the gospel power can help change a family dynamic. The week of James's wedding he had a small breakthrough. He asked his father, "Tell me your thoughts on being a good husband." Neither James, his father, or his mother would necessarily describe his father as a model husband, but James was inviting him to step into a space of health—a space where a father blesses his son and where a man now considers what being a good husband might look like.

James is a close friend of mine and a fellow family systems nerd. He has since reflected on the power of cutoff, "Our entire country's identity is around cutoff. The Boston Tea Party, the War of Independence, the constitutional amendments. America is America by a severe choice to not be with extended family. Our shocking history with Native Americans, African Americans, immigrants. The more I travel the world, the stranger I discover American cutoff is."

In stark contrast to American cutoff, James recently spent time with an Israeli who told him, "We can trace my family line to people who heard Jesus teach." Two thousand years of family history within a twenty-mile radius. It makes you wonder the impact of place and nation on your assumptions about life and God.

Cutoff isn't the only common trait in a genogram. We also see anger being passed down generation to generation, addiction, the power that secrets have to keep us bound. Tragically, physical and sexual abuse is frequently transmitted generation to generation and is one of the most horrific and damaging generational traits. Of course, the power of transmission is also very positive. Genograms also reveal resilience, humor, playfulness, family bonding. The point of a genogram is not to dig up dirt; you may spend some of your genogram celebrating the traits you cherish.

You can get a long way by Googling a genogram to find examples and even instructions on how to build one. A lot of psychology students are required to study and present genograms, so there are all kinds on the internet, including genograms of famous presidents and athletes and even fictional characters. Two fascinating genograms are John F. Kennedy's extended family, with its unusual amount of tragic death that shows up in every generation, and the Skywalker family from Star Wars. GenoPro has a YouTube channel that explains why Luke Skywalker was always so whiny in the first Star Wars movie. You'd be whiny, too, if your father was evil personified and chopped your hand off the first chance he got. It doesn't explain Jar Jar Binks though.

Presenting a genogram is an act of vulnerability. If you choose to present a genogram, you will likely gain some insight about yourself that might be disorienting at first. I encourage you to push through, be kind to yourself, and see what it yields.

HOW TO MAKE A GENOGRAM

1. Get a wide roll of butcher paper, or a flip-chart sized piece of paper and turn it sideways so it is wider than tall.
2. Visit stevecusswords.com to download the free genogram guide for what shapes and patterns to draw.
3. Begin with yourself and any siblings and plot out your family: parents, uncles, aunts, cousins, grandparents, great uncles and aunts, and so forth.

4. Women are drawn as circles. Men are drawn as squares. Put the name inside the circle or square. Connect circles and squares based on their relationship.

5. Plot the emotional relationships. (Again, consult the genogram key.)

6. Check for any missing people. Do you know of any miscarriages or anyone cut off from the family, for example?

Before you begin:

- Some people find it helpful to plot all the relationships out using Post-it Notes before committing to writing on butcher paper. Especially if you have a large extended family, it can be difficult to fit everyone in.

- Use paper with plenty of width and generally begin with yourself in the middle of the paper. If you are the final generation, start at the bottom. If you have a generation or two younger than you, put yourself more in the very center.

- Some people prefer to use a digital app such as GenoPro. It offers all the genogram keys in the app.

- Once you have constructed your genogram, gather your group of trusted friends and lead them through your genogram. Simply begin by telling them about people in your family, starting wherever you like. Presenting a genogram will generally take sixty to ninety minutes, and once you start, your friends can use the question guide below to prompt discussions.

Some final reminders:

- Genograms are not about blame. They are less interested in blame than they are in helping a person discover what she is holding and what is holding her. If you are presenting or listening to a presentation, work to stay focused on awareness, not blame.

- If you do not have an experienced group facilitator who can manage people's vulnerability, or if your own story contains significant trauma or abuse, I recommend hiring a local therapist to come lead your genogram experience. You can still present to your trusted friends, but you'll be grateful to be guided by an experienced group facilitator with some family systems training. Presenting a genogram is always a vulnerable experience and requires a trusted facilitator who is trained in group dynamics and can keep your group on track. For those who are studying these materials in a group, each presenting a genogram, you may choose to hire a therapist to visit your group for several sessions.

- You will almost always run out of time presenting a genogram. The presentation is not about "extracting everything there is to learn." A common reaction to presenting a genogram is, "I wish I had presented _____." You can trust the process and trust that you will continue to gain insight into your family system over time. A genogram is simply a catalyst to ongoing learning.

- A genogram should not be a violating or exploitive experience. You should not have to talk about what you are not ready to talk about. The best genograms are where the presenter is comfortable and safe, but willing to move two or three steps outside his or her own comfort zone.

Genogram questions for group members to ask:
- What themes or questions did you look at in your genogram?
- What patterns do you see?
- What strengths do you see in your family?

- What strengths did you develop out of necessity or were learned?
- Is there anything that surprised you?
- Are there any forgotten people?
- Share two to three adjectives describing key members of your family (angry, joyful, sad, anxious, frustrated, born out of wedlock, grief-ridden, motivated, silly, envious, numb, mental illness, etc.).
- Tell us who had/has the most power in your family. Who had the least? How was power managed?
- Where helpful, tell us the role that someone played in the family. (Some example roles: scapegoat, victim, fixer, favorite, secret keeper, problem solver, baby, screw-up, peacemaker, clown, loser)
- Are there any assumptions you have about life that you'd like to explore or challenge? (i.e., What does your family believe that may not be so?)
- Is there anyone in your family who "broke the family rules"? What happened to that person, and how do you see him or her?
- Is there anything you haven't shared that you'd like to before we finish?

Also, when you are in a group hearing someone present, pay attention to the following:

- The presenter has the power and is in control. Never make a presenter go where he or she is unwilling to go. Pay attention to when the presenter has had enough and respect his or her safety.
- Where did the person begin the presentation? With himself or herself? With a great grandparent? What might this suggest?
- Where did the person spend most of the time?
- Is the presenter giving you "family propaganda" that may not be true? That is, is the presenter teaching the group what life is

about as he or she is presenting the family? Offer the presenter that feedback and gently invite his or her reflection.

- Similarly, is the presenter assuming a universal truth that is not so?
- Pay attention to recurring patterns either in the presenter's family or in his or her presentation. What assumptions does the presenter hold, what kinds of people are he or she judging? Are there any self-fulfilling truths the presenter believes that aren't so?
- Check in on the presenter's capacity at some point. For example, "We've uncovered a lot so far, is this enough, or would you like more? Is there anything we've discussed that you'd like to explore deeper?"
- Close by thanking the person for sharing, offer any encouraging feedback, and pray over the person.

Genograms tend to work on us long after our presentation is done. A good friend will check on a genogram presenter later that day or the next day to see how he or she is doing.

nine

VERBATIMS: KNOWING
HOW YOU SHOW UP

Lord Jesus, let me know myself and know you.
—ST. AUGUSTINE

How many times have you interacted with someone and then thought, *I wish I could do that over again?* Perhaps you were caught off guard by how you came across; you didn't realize what was going on under the surface and you said something you regret. Maybe you struggled to stay engaged with what the other person was saying because of what you were thinking.

Think about the last time you were anxious about a situation or you didn't know what to do. Think about the time you were blindsided by someone or learned that people were talking about you behind your back. What comes to mind when you think of these situations? Is there a way to break through this and find another path?

One of the most powerful tools to help you navigate a fresh way is a *verbatim*. A verbatim is simply a recounting of a previous interaction where you were anxious, or where there was tension or conflict, or you didn't know what to do. The best verbatims are ones where you wish you could do it differently but, of course, you cannot. What you can do though is write up the experience and capture not only what you said and he said, but also what you were thinking and feeling at the time. Once you write it up, you can then print out some copies, grab some trusted friends, and talk through the experience. What was it like? What you were thinking and feeling under the surface?

I have provided some questions at the end of this chapter that your friends or coworkers can use to help you become more aware of what you bring into leadership encounters that you may not be aware of. What triggers you, what assumptions you hold, and so on. While you can never take back that encounter, you can bring your awareness from that encounter into future encounters and show up differently.

You and I have had countless experiences that form us and inform the way we show up. We all push away or avoid specific types of people, we all have triggers that get our minds spinning, we all step on land mines we did not know were there. We have chronic patterns that keep getting us into the same problems every time. This is all completely human and to a large extent will never go away. But once you become aware of your triggers, or the types of people who frustrate you, or your assumptions and chronic behaviors, you now hold a power you did not have before: the power to die to the triggers and assumptions and trust God to lead. As I reflect on my year as a chaplain, it was the experience of presenting dozens of verbatims that helped me most see my tendencies and triggers.

The best verbatim is vivid with detail. You might be thinking that you could never recount, verbatim, an encounter from the past. Who could possibly recall actual word-for-word conversations? I think you would be surprised.

In 1994 I was standing on a dirt road in Jérémie, Haiti, waiting for the bus to take me back to Port-au-Prince. I had spent the week with an incredible missionary family, and as I walked onto the bus I noted that I was surrounded by rural Haitian men and women and a handful of pigs and chickens. Fine travel companions to be sure, but not ones easily communicated with. The bus drove through the night for twelve hours, averaging five miles per hour for most of the journey, switching back and forth up and then down the mountain. The old bus had no lighting and I get queasy on mountain roads. How do you pass the time for twelve hours in such a situation? I recalled one of my college professors tapping his forehead and telling our class, "Everything that you've ever experienced is in there, you just have to get into a space to pull it out. If you spend an hour or two thinking about a situation, you'll be amazed at how much of it you can recall."

I decided to put my professor's thesis to the test. Simply to pass the time on this drive, I tried to recall everything I could remember in my life through school. I began in first grade and made myself put at least twenty minutes into recalling memories and experiences before moving on to the next grade. My brain took a while to come alive, and of course as I moved to later years, I recalled many more vivid memories. After thinking about some years for twenty minutes, I was ready to move on. For other years, I was shocked at how long I could ponder a life experience and recall vivid details, even conversations, from it.

I spent a solid ninety minutes on tenth grade. I could recall in vivid detail our ski trip and also our four-day school backpacking trip. I remembered my semester-long crush on Julia Hamilton and the actual conversation when I finally found the courage to go to her home and ask her out, only to discover she had a boyfriend. I remember sitting in her living room dejected, thinking, *I just wasted an entire semester thinking about this girl and I didn't even do my homework on her relationship status first.* I remember wondering how I should leave when she invited me to stay and offered me apple juice and asked me about my day. No wonder I liked her: she was classy. Sitting on that bus, head on my arm to stave off the motion sickness, I was stunned at how many vivid memories I could recall involving actual dialogue.

It really is true that we retain our experiences; we just sometimes need help unlocking them. If you want to test this theory, you can simply put this book down and sit quietly for fifteen minutes and recall a recent leadership encounter that was difficult. Most likely you can see the environment, recall some dialogue, and maybe even capture what was going on in you when it happened. Thinking on it, you may even relive it somewhat. *

The Bible records verbatim conversations all the time. Because of the recall of Jesus' followers, we actually get to read dialogue between people, and once in a while, the encounter was so profound the author wrote the words of Jesus verbatim in his heart language.

Jesus was navigating a large crowd when Jairus elbowed and excused his way to the front, begging Jesus to come heal his daughter. Jesus agreed, and after stopping to help a couple of folks along the way, he approached the house. The neighbors flagged him down and said he was too late; the little girl had died. Jesus replied coolly, "She is not dead but asleep" (Luke 8:52) and proceeded to ignore the mocking crowd and enter the house. Jesus walked right into the little girl's

---

* A quick note to people to who have navigated trauma in your life: I do not recommend doing a verbatim involving a trauma encounter outside the care of a trusted therapist. The goal of a verbatim is to help you grow in self-awareness of your triggers and thoughts and feelings. But for those recovering from trauma, it will not be helpful outside a therapist's care.

room, took the child by the hand, and said, *"Talitha koum!"* which means "Little girl, I say to you, get up!"

This story is recorded in chapter 5 of Mark's gospel. His entire gospel was written in Greek except for this occasion and a couple of others in which he quoted verbatim the words of Jesus in Aramaic. The New Testament Gospels were all written in Greek because it was the most widespread language of the time, but Jesus and his disciples spoke Aramaic because that was their heart language. It is somewhat like a first generation Hispanic family speaking English at work or school and Spanish in the home. The first is the language of the culture, the second is the language of the family's heart. Greek was the language of the culture; Aramaic was the language of the heart. Why did Mark record a portion of this encounter in Aramaic? Why did he write, *"Talitha koum"*? Why not just write, "Jesus said, 'Little girl, I say to you, get up'"?

Because he was recording the experience verbatim.

Mark was Peter's assistant, so his gospel is Peter's recollection of encounters with Jesus. Mark never actually met Jesus, he only wrote about Jesus from Peter's experience. As I imagine it, Peter was recounting for Mark his life with Jesus, and as often happens, he was reliving the encounter as he was retelling it. I can imagine Peter getting more and more excited as he retold this story to Mark, his words getting faster, using one long run-on sentence: "And Jesus went to heal the girl but it was too late, she was already dead, but Jesus said she wasn't dead and that's when we knew something was about to happen, because with Jesus you just never knew when something amazing was about to happen, and sure enough, he walks right into her room, takes her by the hand, and says, '*Talitha koum.*'"

And then a breath.

"I will never forget those words as long as I live."

That's what happens when you retell some experiences—the person who had the experience and the listeners are all back in it. To put us right in the room with Jesus and Peter, Mark left the words verbatim in the original spoken language. Of course, Peter didn't speak to Mark in English and have him write in Aramaic. He more likely spoke in Aramaic or in Greek to Mark, but all the same, I am suggesting Mark left key memories in Aramaic because they had a profound impact and captured a moment. He did it again in Mark 7 where some people brought their deaf and mute friend to Jesus for healing. They asked Jesus to lay hands on the man, but Jesus did them one better by sticking his finger in the man's ear and grabbing the man's tongue! Jesus then offered a one-word prayer, and Mark kept it in the Aramaic, "*Ephphatha!*' (which means 'Be opened!')" (v. 34). I would imagine Peter was getting used to Jesus healing people by this point, but Jesus shocked Peter by using a rather invasive healing procedure! Peter was stunned by his master and recounted the experience as such. I imagine he said to Mark, "He stuck his finger in the guy's ear and then spat and grabbed the guy's tongue! And then he prayed, 'Ephphatha!'"

Finally, we can all imagine how deeply Peter was impacted by his master's death on the cross, which might be why, as he retold the event to Mark, he almost whispered Jesus' words, *"Eloi, Eloi, lema sabachthani?"* which means "My God, my God, why have you forsaken me?" (Mark 15:34).

Verbatim.

Some experiences have such a profound impact that you can recall them in vivid detail, and in recalling them you almost relive the experience. This is the type of experience we examine in a verbatim. A verbatim is a three- to five-page written account and analysis of a leadership experience you recently had. You capture, as best as you can remember, actual dialogue from the encounter, as well as what you were thinking and feeling leading up to the encounter and what you were thinking and feeling during the encounter. You conclude a verbatim document with a summary of what you observe about it upon reflection and also where you see or don't see God at work in it. I have links to sample verbatims at the end of the chapter that will help you with verbatim page layout and category.

A verbatim offers a leader the rare gift of being able to revisit a leadership encounter to learn from it and grow for the next one. The goal of a verbatim is not to "do it better next time" and certainly not to have a mulligan. The goal is to be aware of how you show up in leadership encounters and what is going on in you under the surface. The best way to utilize a verbatim is in a small, trusted group setting where one person presents a verbatim encounter and the other people help her or him process what he or she was thinking and feeling during the encounter.

All of us carry experiences and anxieties that inform our worldview and most certainly inform how we show up in leadership. We bring to every encounter a set of assumptions and wounds, or maybe something as simple as a bad day, and all of these form us under the surface of our awareness and infect our leadership ability. By examining these in a verbatim, we are able to grow in awareness of how the self can get in the way of being fully present to God and the people we are called to serve and lead. Instead of being triggered and reactive, we can be freer to serve the person in front of us, even if that person is hostile or frustrates us or throws a curve ball our way. By going through several verbatim experiences, we become less reactive and better able to serve and lead. This is not nearly as easy as I make it sound, but it is a journey well worth taking.

Years ago, I was leading a local group of pastors in a verbatim when Chris walked in looking a bit sheepish, copies of his verbatim in hand. Chris is very easygoing and certainly not a person who is easily riled, but he had lost his temper while typing up his verbatim the night before. One of his leadership goals for the year was to explore why he lets people roll over him and how to appropriately exert his leadership power without rolling over others. His verbatim was an encounter from a few years before at a different ministry organization.

He had been promised a promotion, and he typed up the encounter of the meeting where he learned that he would not be getting the promised promotion. His manager was there, as was another director. They had promised him the role but then gave it to an out-of-state friend. Rather than simply be honest with Chris, they blamed the lack of promotion on areas Chris needed to work on, including one particular area that was not accurate yet tapped into one of his fears.

We've all seen leadership encounters where a leader makes a mistake (in this case promising a role and then not keeping that promise), and rather than own the mistake the leader hangs it on an employee. We all try to cover our shame in various ways, and this is a particularly insidious way. But what made this encounter more insidious is how it played exactly to Chris's fears that he was too easily rolled over. Should he express anger and power up? It was not in his nature to do so, yet it was the very thing he struggled with. A promotion has very tangible family implications of finances and future. This event had occurred a long time ago at a different organization, but when Chris was typing his verbatim the evening before in his home, all those emotions and anxieties rose up again, and he surprised himself when he suddenly hit the boiling point and threw his cell phone against the wall.

Let's take Chris's story a couple of steps further. What got Chris's blood boiling in this meeting (and when he typed it up several years later) was his deep fear that his easygoing personality makes him a pushover. Yet it is not his nature to be aggressive, so he was in a double bind, and all his history in being passed over or pushed around came to a head in this one encounter. Chris was no longer simply dealing with the facts of this one encounter, he was bringing his past into his present, and his past was now dictating his present behavior. Often our future is also in play in these situations as we wonder if we can ever change some of the deep-seated fears and traits we have known about but cannot dislodge. A verbatim offered Chris the gift of reexploring a painful encounter in a safe environment where he could hold his assumptions and triggers rather than them holding him. If you do enough verbatims, you will be able to pay attention to these triggers as they are happening. In this way, you manage them rather than the triggers managing you.

When I was a hospital chaplain, one of the ongoing challenges was staying fully present to people as their loved ones were dying. While on some days nobody in the hospital died, on other days I attended to four or five deaths. After a long overnight shift and multiple deaths, no one wants more death. Early in my chaplaincy I was not aware of what was going on under the surface as I would walk into a room to attend to a grieving family or a person actively dying. But as I went through the verbatim experience every week, I became much more attuned to what I was thinking and feeling, and the results were frankly quite startling. I have already mentioned the prayer I prayed every time I walked to the ER for an incoming trauma patient. Here are a few other examples of what I discovered under the surface of my life:

- After three deaths in a day, I sat in the staff break room eating my chuck wagon steak and watching *Seinfeld* reruns because they were a distraction from pain and death. My pager beeped and I was called to attend a fourth death. I walked into the room angry at the family for interrupting the *Seinfeld* rerun. I thought to myself, *I can stay in the room for ten minutes, offer a scripture from Philippians, wrap it up with a prayer, and get back to the Seinfeld rerun.* I am, of course, not proud of this thought, but at the same time, it is a very human thought. Presenting it in a verbatim to my fellow chaplains helped me die to it and ask God to use me to be fully present to this freshly grieving family who need guidance and care.
- After several months of horror and trauma, I was called upon to visit a distraught wife of a heart attack victim. She wanted me to pray for her husband. Earlier she found him slumped over his dinner at the dining table, and now he was in the ER

on a heart monitor. He was alert and had no open wounds or tubes coming out of him. I was frustrated at being bothered by such a relatively minor request. I looked at the wife, who was deeply distraught, and I thought to myself, *You think you've got problems? How about I take you to some people who are in really bad shape?* Of course, she has every right to be deeply distraught after her husband suddenly collapsed, but my private mental response was one of exhaustion from a chaplain who has seen too much trauma and was numbing to it.

No, I did not say any of these thoughts out loud, but in my first few months of chaplaincy, I was not aware I was even thinking these thoughts. I had been raised and then trained in a church tradition that did not make room for these types of thoughts because they are "un-Christlike." Yes, they are un-Christlike. They are also human and natural. Each of these thoughts held the common theme of keeping a safe distance from death and tragedy. I wrote more than sixty verbatims during my chaplaincy, and through the months I grew more and more aware of what was going on under the surface. Because of the care of my small group of chaplains and supervisors, I felt less and less threatened by exposing these thoughts. I was able to pay attention to my assumptions: that a "real Christian" should never think such things, that I should always be "on," and others.

Through the verbatim process, I became acutely aware of when I was tired or angry at death or afraid that a patient would be someone I love. As I walked into a room not knowing what to expect, I was able to offer my thoughts and feelings to God and die to them. *Lord, I am tired of death, but these people need a chaplain who can be present and attentive and serve them well. I want to run away and finish quickly, so I die to that desire and I trust that you will strengthen me to serve them. Help me to be attentive to your Spirit and your people in this next encounter.* Twenty years later my context is different, but that dynamic is exactly the same. Leadership is an onslaught of challenge and it can take a toll. If we are not aware of what is going on under the surface, we become bound by it.

A verbatim helps you to notice the ways that false self gets in the way, so you can die to it and be more present to people. And once again, easier written than done. All of these tools—the sources of anxiety, the genogram, the verbatim—none of them will stop you from thinking these thoughts, experiencing these triggers. The gift they offer is not to remove these thoughts but to notice them as they arise, and to offer them to God as a living sacrifice. Without these tools, our triggers and the stories we tell ourselves make us sacrifice through anxiety and fear. These tools diffuse the power anxiety has over us.

A chaplain dealing with death is a particularly intense example, to be sure, but since that time I have helped leaders verbatim elders' meetings, conflicts with fellow staff, difficult customers, all manner of people and situations. A verbatim does not need the high stakes of death and trauma to work; it simply needs anxiety and challenging or chronic repeated behavior. As a lead pastor, I think the same "human-level" thoughts as I did when I was a chaplain. The fantasy fight with the uninvolved critic who is technically right in his criticism, the need to hear, "That was the best sermon ever" after every sermon, the fear of pressure as the church grows and the organization gets more complex. The list is endless.

Genevieve went into a children's team meeting excited to share her new vision and plans for a worship ministry. She was a young leader, newer to the church and still getting to know the volunteers. As she wrapped up the meeting, she noticed the team's demeanor changed significantly. Genevieve was confused that what she thought would be a time of excitement became a time of pain. She had stepped on a land mine in the room and didn't know it was there. This encounter is verbatim gold.

Quinn manages a large home improvement chain store. He is a

Christian who takes seriously his leadership in a corporate setting. One of his shift workers has been showing up chronically late, always having a different excuse and making it hard on the other workers. Quinn has noticed that even though his employee is the one in the wrong, Quinn is always the one paying for it. He knows he needs to confront his employee, but Quinn struggles to confront people and doesn't know why. Other employees have noticed the chronically late coworker is getting away with it, and when they've talked to Quinn about it, he's gotten defensive and has told them to mind their own business. This is verbatim gold.

All leaders experience stepping on land mines with groups of people and causing unintentional pain. All leaders have experienced bringing a wound into a meeting and acting out of it, or holding assumptions about specific people and then seeing the world through those assumptions, reinforcing them. All leaders have chronic patterns that shrink their leadership reach and ability.

A verbatim doesn't eliminate land mines or wounds or assumptions, it simply allows a leader a safe environment to become more aware of them and therefore be able to manage them in future leadership encounters. A verbatim gives a leader the incredible gift of self-examination so that the leader can then choose to die to that aspect of self and see if God has a better, more freeing reality than the one the leader assumed.

Our leadership community makes everyone do at least one verbatim, and we always receive highly positive feedback from the experience. If you'd like to see a classic verbatim from clinical pastoral education, you can look at these links:

- http://chaplainsreport.com/2014/05/06/sample-cpe-verbatim-allowing-for-authenticity/
- http://chaplainsreport.com/2013/08/29/another-sample-cpe-verbatim-depression-and-significance/

HOW TO WRITE A VERBATIM

Never use full names (identify people by initials), respect confidentiality and discretion. If you are in a smaller leadership environment, you may all know who is featured in which case; discretion rather than confidentiality is the goal. Double-space between passages of speech.

VERBATIM LOGISTICS AND LAYOUT

A verbatim will take one to three hours to write up, and in the end will be between three to seven pages in length, depending on the length of your encounter. Here is how to lay it out:

1. Introduction

Provide the date and time length of the encounter. Provide a paragraph helping to set the scene. What were you walking into? How were you feeling at the time? What were you aware of in yourself? What was on your mind before this interaction? Were you aware of any anxiety or excitement? Was there anything that was unrelated to the experience that may have affected your behavior during this experience? Are there sociocultural or other factors that may have influenced how you processed this verbatim (language, economic, racial, or ethnic differences, age, education, and so forth)? What motivated your responses in this particular situation?

Total length should be one to four paragraphs.

2. Verbatim

The actual verbatim is a two-column table. On the left is the actual dialogue between you and the person or people. Using their initials, label them L1, L2, and L3 for each time L speaks. Capture everyone's actual speech as best you remember it. Under each dialogue, capture nonverbal communication in brackets, including pauses, periods of silence, and so forth.

On the right column, lined with the speech, do your best to capture what you were thinking and feeling at the time. As you reflect back on the encounter, what triggered you? What went through your mind? Do your best to be aware of how you were during the actual encounter. Note: it is common to not recall every single word, or even the entire interaction, just capture as much as you can remember. Also, just like a genogram, a verbatim is not intended to be an objective record of an encounter. It is a tool to help you become more aware of how you show up in an encounter.

The verbatim length is mostly determined by the length of the conversation: two to five pages.

3. Post-Encounter Reflection

What are you aware of now that you may not have been aware of at the time? A verbatim is another tool to help you "think about the way you think," so as you revisit your encounter, you may notice patterns and behaviors and thoughts. Capture those here.

Total length is one to three paragraphs.

4. Theological Analysis

What assumptions do you and the people in the verbatim have about God? Was God openly discussed? What does the encounter reveal about the human condition? Sin? Structural evil? Grace? What does this encounter say about vocation? What course of action is fitting following this situation? What aspects of your own faith were explored, challenged, or reaffirmed?

Total length is one to three paragraphs.

FINAL REFLECTION

Now that you have reentered this experience, what faith response is called for by you or by the others involved? What have you learned from this experience? What might you be able to do to help this person grow socially, emotionally, or spiritually? How did you or will you follow up on this situation?

A NOTE TO GROUP LEADERS

Good questions to ask:

- Why did you pick this encounter?
- Could you give a description of her/him?
- What would you like us to help you with?
- What were you thinking?
- What are you feeling?
- Please define anxiety.
- Is there a reason why you shifted here?
- Tell us about (a person in the verbatim).
- What assumptions do you what to examine?
- What recurring behaviors have you noticed that you'd like to explore?

A verbatim is best processed in a trusted small group with an appointed group leader. A verbatim will typically take forty-five to sixty minutes to process. If your group is processing more than one verbatim in a session, be aware that the "presenter" will struggle to be fully present during the next verbatim. Presenting a verbatim takes an emotional toll!

Most people will move into shame when they present a verbatim. We all naturally regret the way we do things, and when our mistakes are laid out in front of others, we naturally feel the need to hide. The group leader's primary job is to pay attention to the presenter's shame and the rest of the group's desire to "fix" or advise on how it should have been done. The simplest way to help is to name both of these tendencies, thank the presenter for his or her courage and vulnerability, and affirm areas that are difficult.

For example, I remember my first verbatim, which was the encounter I described in chapter 1 of this book: my first encounter with death and grief. I wrote the verbatim thinking that experts would know how to do this better, and the experts in my verbatim group were very kind to me, telling me over and again, "This is one of those situations where no one ever knows what to do and no amount of experience helps." If the presenter is sharing a common struggle, you can serve that person by identifying that you would struggle too.

ESSENTIAL GROUP LEADER TOOLS

- It is most helpful to set ground rules before the presenter starts.
- No advice. No mothering. No teaching. No "Here's how you could have done it." Only questions to help the person become more aware of himself or herself.
- Invite the person to consider taking a step or two beyond his or her comfort zone. A verbatim isn't intended to tear someone down or make the person feel he or she is free falling. Pay attention to how much feedback a person can take before he or she needs a break.
- Make sure no one in your group is featured in another person's verbatim; it makes a verbatim weird.

- Protect the presenter from shame. We will make mistakes or wish we had done things different. You can serve the presenter by gently reminding her or him that a verbatim is not about perfection or regret.

- Oddly, groups can sometimes subconsciously reenact the verbatim. Pay attention to whether your group is reenacting the situation.

- Finally, and perhaps most important: some personalities struggle to define what they are feeling at any given time. If the presenter is frequently answering, "I don't know" to the question "What was going through your mind when this happened?" then honor the person and don't push for more.

ten

A WIDER SCOPE AND
A DEEPER CAPACITY

*If you want to build a ship, don't drum up the men to
gather wood, divide the work, and give orders. Instead,
teach them to yearn for the vast and endless sea.*
—ANTOINE DE SAINT-EXUPÉRY

The vision for this model of leadership is a culture where people can bring their whole selves and hold one another's vulnerability in a caring way, where we can name and move through our shadows, vows, and anxieties to be more fully present to one another and to God.

Scores of leadership books use a model of inspiration and coercion, but getting somebody amped up for a cause or making someone do something he or she does not want to do takes very little skill. It also doesn't last. This approach is slower and messier but builds a culture that outlasts the leader and, most important, allows a person to bring his or her whole self to the organization or family. But it takes time to see the impact.

In 2004, after years of battling chronic lower back pain and looking into all manner of options, including surgery, I visited a local chiropractor who had a reputation of being a miracle worker. I was quite skeptical, especially since people gave him such glowing reviews. My back pain had been debilitating at times, to the point of my being bedridden, and I didn't think anything outside of surgery could help. In the initial consultation I asked, "Do I have to believe to be healed?" He laughed and replied that his approach did not depend on belief or mental gymnastics. He would either heal me or he wouldn't, but the healing was based on science and my physiology, not placebo and psychosomatics. But he added, "You won't know if you're better for several months. I will see you three times per week for six weeks, and then your treatment will be done. You will likely still be in significant pain at the end of the treatment period, but if the treatment works, you'll be pain free after six to nine months."

Sure enough, I hobbled out of my final appointment in as much pain as I brought in, but slowly, imperceptibly at first, my pain subsided and I was able to do more without that dreaded spasm. About eight months later I woke up realizing that for the first time in a couple of years, I was pain free. I became a believer.

This material is quite like that—you may be done with the book, but that doesn't mean your anxiety is controlled or quelled. If you begin a habit of trying these tools, you will slowly discover a level of freedom and peace that you didn't have before. For many of us, it takes years.

Transformation takes time and involves a lot of failure. In order to go through this process, you have to become good at forgiving yourself. Particularly for perfectionists, this process can be challenging. Once you try some of the tools, you will see recurring patterns in your own life, but will not immediately change them. You might even move into shame and condemnation by mistakenly thinking, *I should know better by now.* But the self you discover through these tools is long forged and deeply entrenched. You've been relying on this self to get you through some pretty tough seasons your whole life. Transformation and dying to self takes time, and you need to be kind to yourself through the process.

In the United States, professional baseball players are paid huge amounts of money, even though most often their time at bat results in an out. A perfect batting average is 1.000. If a player averages .300, he's considered exceptional and gets paid millions of dollars. Paradoxically, .300 means he gets a base hit only about three times out of ten trips to the plate. It isn't even about hitting a home run every time at bat, it is simply about getting to first base. So, professional baseball players are worth millions of dollars per year to their teams even if they do not get on base seven out of ten times. If they can be paid millions for failing twice as often as they succeed, you can be kind to yourself for going down the old path now that you know better, and you can relax into the knowledge that growth takes time, prayer, and practice.

Jeremiah is one of my favorite Old Testament writers because he wrote before and during the Exile, one of the most forging experiences in the life of God's people. God instructed Jeremiah to buy a field (Jer. 32). It made little sense because the people were about to be exiled. Babylon would lay to waste all the farms and buildings, and the place would be desolate for a few generations. But Jeremiah obeyed God, bought a field, and gave the deed to one of his assistants. God was basically saying, "I know things are about to get worse, but on the other side of that, this field will produce all manner of abundant fruit." Jeremiah's purchase was about knowing that fruit would come to that field after a difficult season.

I sometimes feel the same way about these materials. Things may get worse in the short term as you disrupt status quo within yourself and your organization, but on the other side is immense fruit provided by the goodness of God. I encourage you to set your face like flint toward the healing and freedom the gospel promises, even if you are under siege right now.

In leadership, learning happens best after the encounter. One of the most disorienting aspects of chaplaincy was how the supervisors refused to educate us before an encounter. They gave no instruction on grief, death protocol, staff issues, not to mention my own internal issues. Much like Jesus did to the disciples in Luke 9, they sent us out ill-equipped and then debriefed with us when we returned. As you look at Jesus' model in Luke 9, not only did he send out the disciples on a mission, but he stripped them of their comforts and securities before they left. They went out with nothing other than God's presence and their wits. When they returned, Jesus sat down and heard all about what they had done and what God had done through them.

That is the model I was trained in while a chaplain, and it is the basis of these tools. You will step out feeling ill-equipped, try some tools, and then debrief over and over again. After about six weeks of chaplaincy I got the hang of the lack of safety net and learned to walk by faith—trusting that God would guide me and that my mistakes would do less damage than I feared.

I think leadership development operates this same way: we can take a class and read a book, but real development comes when we dive in over our heads, try some things, and adjust as we go. We learn more by doing it and reflecting on it than we do by reading about it or being told about it then doing it. As you navigate some of the tools in this book, I encourage you to find situations where you don't know what to do, move into them, and then reflect on the experience. Some of you are adventure junkies and will happily jump off any cliff into the unknown; others are more cautious. Either way, all of us can measure our comfort zones and then move two or three steps beyond our comfort into uncharted territory. Uncharted for us, that is. God has been there all along, waiting for us. You're going to make mistakes and take some licks and beatings along the way. I know of no leader who has spent even a few years in leadership without being burned or wounded. It comes with the territory.

Chris Seidman wrote, "A while back I was talking with a professional athlete who belongs to our church. He was in the midst of his twelfth NBA season. It was the morning after a game. He was walking rather stiff. I asked him if he was hurt. He said, 'No, at this point in the season most everyone at this level is playing through some kind of pain.' Those words have bounced around in my spirit for a while. This is true when it comes to ministry over the long haul. Now there are times when we need to rest, withdraw, or retreat. We all know the importance of observing some kind of Sabbath rhythm. After all, you can't fill a moving cup. But there are times in our lives when we have to play hurt."[1]

I have studied leadership for two decades, and I am privileged to be friends with many leaders. As I swap stories and battle scars with my friends, and as I read and listen to well-known leaders, I discover common themes and experiences that each leader shares. Could it be that God creates leaders through the same common experiences?

The First Common Experience: The Leader Is Ill-Equipped for the Task at Hand at a Young Age

This was my experience as a chaplain and as a lead pastor, and as I reflect on it, most of my leadership endeavors. It might be your story as well. You were thrust into leadership before you were ready. You were ill-equipped and had to figure it out. Not only that but you had to lead people to a place you'd never been yourself, maybe even people who knew better than you. You made mistakes along the way, you'd do it different now, and you often say, "If I only knew then . . ." But all the same you learned how to lead a group of people into the unknown. If this isn't your story and you want to grow as a leader, find something you don't know how to do and lead it. All manner of anxieties will arise from that experience, forging you into deeper leadership.

Our church invites college students to serve with us for a year or two as interns. They take their classes online and spend twenty hours a week working for the church. They go through the class that is the basis of this book, but they also do several "hard skills," and one of them is leading something they don't know how to do. It can be almost anything, so long as we need it and they don't know how to do it.

One of our interns built a prayer labyrinth on our property for us. He didn't know anything about labyrinths, the materials needed to build one, architecture, or the political process to navigate—none of it. As an intern he led our executive pastor (who has a masters in project management), our project manager (who has a masters in landscape architecture), as well as a host of volunteers, city staff, and other people in the implementation of this vision. Everyone he led is older than him and knows more than he does about the process. He had to "figure it out" in front of more experienced people and lead them in this overall project.

All leaders I respect have been thrust, sometimes again and again, into the unknown and had to figure it out. If you want to grow as a leader, or if you want to learn more about your internal anxieties and triggers, find something you know nothing about that is needed by an organization and offer to lead it.

The Second Common Experience: The Leader Is Burned by the Organization She or He Loves

In my case, the organization is the church, and being burned by the church is one of the harshest burning experiences because we put so much hope in what the church should be. When the church falls short, which it always will, the experience hurts more. But the obvious reality is that the church, or any faith-based organization, is full of imperfect people and imperfect leaders whose mistakes cause real damage. I've been damaged by the church; you probably have too. But here is the lesser discussed reality: I've damaged the church, and you may have too.

I won't go into detail about the burning I received from a church I served; suffice to say that the person who burned me made the front page of the newspaper for fraud and deceit. But this is also true: I did not behave honorably through the burning process. I would like to posit myself as a pure victim in the burn, and by all external accounts, I could spin that story. But my heart knows another story: I gossiped, I exaggerated, I spoke poorly of people behind their backs. I did not act above reproach as I was being burned.

I don't for a moment compare our stories to Joseph from the Old Testament, but as I read his story I marvel at how loosely he held his circumstance and how tightly I hold mine. Joseph took his burns as part of a larger plan, but I think we naturally take ours as a grave injustice. They are an injustice, of course, but they are also an opportunity for God to forge us. As much as I want to demonize the person who burned me and as much as I don't think he should be in ministry, I also have to admit that I learned a great deal from him. I wasn't as honorable as my imagination thinks, and without that painful burn, I would not be at the church I serve now.

Some people have not only been burned, they have also been abused. Abuse and trauma are a different territory beyond the scope of what I'm writing here. Some have been wounded to an extent that professional and legal help is needed. I am not implying that the abused should go back to the abuser, quite the opposite. Emotional and physical safety are paramount, especially for an abuse survivor.

But many of us were not abused, we were burned. And in our

attempt to heal we became self-righteous. The pain you experienced from your burn is real, but hopefully it can open you to a wider, more nuanced and healing understanding. One of my great comforts as I was working through being burned was discovering how this burning process is such a common experience among church leaders I respect. It helped me to reframe the burning as a "forging" that many people go through, and this was freeing for me. It helped me forgive the very human and broken people, many of whom are good people and many of whom I did not honor when things were getting rough.

The Third Common Experience: Leaders Have to Reinvent Their Approach to Their Organizations Constantly

When I first started leading in my current church, I had two staff and a volunteer board. Now I have thirty staff, a volunteer board, and a spin-off nonprofit. I have entirely reinvented the way I lead three or four times over the past decade as our organization has grown. Dennis Bratton, a friend of mine who served local churches for more than forty years, took me aside a few years ago and said, "Once your staff gets above ten people, you will always have trouble." If I didn't trust Dennis, I would not have taken his wisdom seriously—it was a broad-brush generalization, but he was right.

Not that our staff is a problem, but at any given moment at least one in ten people face a significant struggle that debilitates or heavily affects their leadership and requires attention.

Not only does our organization change, but our context changes. I am currently pastoring an organizational church in an era where organizations are being deconstructed. Suspicion toward organizational leaders and especially religious leaders is at an all-time high, and much of that suspicion is unfortunately well-earned. Also, by all data metrics I am middle-aged. I don't feel middle-aged, but I sit with some of our millennial staff and discover that the way I think and how I see the world is significantly different from how they think and how they view the world.

Not only do I adjust for the size of our organization, but I adjust to the changing context of our ministry. And let's face it, millennials are becoming the older edge of young people. Here come the centennials! I know of no respected leader who isn't constantly learning and adjusting to the times and what the organization requires. Lifelong leadership requires constant shedding and adapting, growing and learning from all manner of people, including people half your age.

So, the common denominators of leaders I respect: we've all been thrown into the deep end before we were taught to swim, we've all been burned by the organizations we love, and we've all had to adjust to the ever-changing reality of our times and organizations. Knowing this does not make it any easier, but it rightsizes my expectations, helps me look for opportunities that challenge my comfort and skill level, and gives me perspective when things are going south.

For a Christian leader, leadership is actually about followership. Paul provocatively wrote to the church in Corinth, "Follow my example, as I follow the example of Christ" (1 Cor. 11:1), and for years that really bugged me. It felt so arrogant of Paul. I wish he'd written, "Follow Christ as I follow Christ with you," or something less preposterous than "Follow me." But Paul intentionally placed himself between the Corinthian people and Christ. Why?

When Jesus was on earth, following him was certainly not easy, but it was straightforward. No doubt, Jesus said things and went places that kept the disciples scratching their collective heads and saying among themselves, "It's your turn to ask. I asked him last time and I still feel like an idiot." As far as I can tell, Peter was the appointed, or perhaps self-appointed, disciple to take a deep breath and say to Jesus, "I don't get it."

Jesus left his followers perplexed as often as not. So following Jesus certainly was no afternoon stroll, but it was pretty basic. Following

Jesus back then was physical as much as it was spiritual. If you wanted to follow Jesus, you just had to walk alongside him or behind him. If you saw Jesus far off and you were one of his followers, all you had to do was walk up to him and wait for what was next, and you'd be following him effectively. Following Jesus was a literal act of proximity, even when he was asking you to do something outrageous.

But when Jesus ascended into heaven and the Holy Spirit came down, following Jesus became a lot less tangible. Where is Jesus now? He's sort of everywhere. How do I follow Jesus now? Well, you remember his teaching and you follow his Holy Spirit. Who is to say what the Holy Spirit is saying?

Fast-forward two thousand years and we have ten thousand denominations disagreeing on what it looks like to follow Jesus and the Holy Spirit. No wonder Paul said, "Follow my example, as I follow the example of Christ" to the Corinthian people. None of them had much of an idea about how to follow Jesus and they needed a model. When you have to tell someone, "You really shouldn't be sleeping with your stepmother" and "Stop elbowing your way to the front of the communion line," they're basically without a clue. But Paul knew how to follow Jesus and I think Paul was saying, "Follow me. I'll be a tangible model of what following Christ looks like and you'll get there."

Healthy leaders should also say, "Follow me." Not arrogantly, and of course not in place of people following Jesus for themselves, but as a model. It is another way of saying virtuous leaders go first, and the first thing virtuous leaders do is follow Jesus. I state this rather obvious point because we all know Christian leaders whose followership is dangerously disconnected from their leadership. In the quest for more and better, they left behind actually following Jesus long ago. One of the strongest temptations a leader will face is to allow a growing gap between her leadership and followership. In many ways, this gap is more insidious than power issues or sexual struggles because a leader can be promoted into higher levels of leadership while his own followership stays stunted. By modeling after Paul and recognizing that our own following of Jesus is directly tied to our leadership capacity, we can help keep that gap minimized.

PLATFORM, GIFTING, AND THE GOSPEL

The authority by which the Christian leader leads is not power but love, not force but example, not coercion but reasoned persuasion. Leaders have power, but power is safe only in the hands of those who humble themselves to serve.
—JOHN STOTT

Paul's writing to the Corinthian church was culturally radical. His message was that every single person has equal importance and contribution in the church even though they do very different functions and even though some are seen and some are unseen. Consider for a moment the Roman Empire and the way power and hierarchy worked in Rome. Contrast that to Paul's vision for the church. No wonder people flocked in droves to church in the first three hundred years of history—it was the first place where a cultural nobody is now a somebody. It was civil rights before civil rights became a thing.

Paul was saying. "In the empire, you have no status and you're lowly. In the kingdom of God, you are somebody and you are no more or less somebody than the person beside you." The preacher and nursery worker are on equal footing in the church. The quiet mechanic who helps repair cars of single parents is just as vital as the vocalist who can move crowds to tears. I think this power has been lost in the last twenty-five years of leadership teaching in the church.

In the 1980s, churches desperately needed leadership development training, and for the next two decades plenty of skilled leaders gave us great resources. But like all overcorrections, we may have swung the pendulum too far. I wonder if we have forgotten Paul's vision for the body of Christ amid our need for leadership development. We have overemphasized leadership above other gifts and we have given too much attention to a narrow type of leader. We have focused on type A, high D, high I charismatic leaders with strong communication skills. The church needs these leaders in droves but no more than other types of leaders and other types of followers who are not leaders.

Our church culture is littered with highly driven and gifted leaders who have crashed and dropped out, or more commonly stepped away for a while, avoided accountability, and stepped right back into the spotlight of public leadership. The wake of damage left behind by unhealthy, highly driven leaders is stunning. What we need are healthy leaders of all stripes and healthy non-leaders who each together serve the body of Christ.

LEADING FROM GIFTING VERSUS LEADING FROM PLATFORM

What is the difference between Christian leadership and other forms of leadership? I believe the difference comes down to platform versus gifting. So often we follow people because of platform when we should be following because of gifting.

When I was in graduate school, I worked as a day laborer to earn some extra money over Christmas break. I reported to the office the first morning at 5:30 and they assigned me to a crew who was constructing a dock over a lake for a nearby hospital. The work was good and the guys on the team were easy to get along with. But it was also a fascinating experience of hierarchy and middle management because there was one guy who never did any work. He just sat in his truck, drank coffee and possibly some additives, and watched us work. He was the site superintendent. Every day he would show up late to the site, sit in his pickup, and read the paper, and occasionally he would come down to check on us. When he did surprise us with his presence, his primary goal was to clarify that he was the boss and we were the schmucks. We were doing all the work, including reading the blueprints and figuring out the procedure, but he was making the most money. The reason I knew that is because he liked to tell us.

Not exactly a model leader.

He also didn't know us. He didn't care to get to know us so he didn't know what we had to offer. If one of the men had injured himself and ended up inside the hospital, overlooking the lake and almost dock, I had the experience to visit and help. But he never mined us for our gifts and unique contributions—he just saw us as a blob of generic humanity from whom to extract labor. But that is so often the way of the world. What this guy did was nothing unusual. It happens in workplaces and PTAs and even within marriages all over the world.

But it should not be so with us. The temptation of every person who wants to make an impact is to wish we were like somebody else. We look at the gifts and talents of another person and we think, *If I had those gifts, I'd be a better leader,* but God has made each of us unique and qualified to lead based on our gifting. In the church people ought not follow because "she is in charge" but because of her gifting.

One simple exercise for those brave enough to try it is to ask people you trust, "Why do people follow me?" If you gather several friends and ask one another, you will discover a variety of differences. We follow Beth because of the way she makes the Bible come alive. We follow Andrew because of his passion for the cause. Chris has this unique ability to create a safe space just by his posture and tone. John inspires us to try things we didn't think we could do. Shelly quietly comes alongside and ushers us forward with very particular encouragement. Healthy leadership operates out of gifting, not platform, so it operates regardless of your status in the organization.

The day I make people follow me "because I'm lead pastor, that's why" is the day I lose leadership capital with my people. My platform, lead pastor, is the conduit of my leadership—it is how I deliver my leadership, but it is not the source of my leadership. The source of my leadership is God and the gifts he has given me, and while some people follow me because of my platform, most follow because of my gifting, and the same is true for you too. This is why some people can have a huge impact without an official platform—just their very personality and gifting is why you follow them. Title becomes almost irrelevant. So, for the Christian leader, authority to lead comes from gifts, not the title on the business card, and none of us is more important than the other in the organization.

I would like to close with the same reminder I began with. While many leaders can benefit greatly from these tools, some have faced significant trauma, and others fight a mental illness. For those people: your trauma or your illness does not disqualify you from ministry. According to Paul in 2 Corinthians 1, it may uniquely qualify you to minister to people I could never reach. But also, you may require a fundamental level of care beyond the scope of this book. A therapist or a psychiatrist may be your next step, even if you have tried them before. Neither of those mean you are weak or less spiritual, but a trusted, skilled therapist and psychiatrist can provide a baseline foundation for you to begin to heal.

At a recent class on these materials one of our group facilitators, Jimmy, told the group, "This is hard work, but staying the same and not doing this work is hard too. It is just that you are familiar with the 'hard' you're in now. You've become so accustomed to the anxiety you carry every day that you don't realize how hard it is." I think Jimmy named a real dynamic at play in this sort of work. You will try some of these tools and bumble through. It will take several months or more to pay attention to process and content. You will walk down old familiar paths that you thought you were done with. But if you keep at it, invite others into this way, move toward health, and fight for freedom, I promise you will see fruit on the other side.

As I have previously mentioned, many of these concepts take years to fully integrate, especially if you've been entrenched for some time. In many cases, you will not be able to change a challenging relationship, you will only be able to manage your own reaction to it. Many of the concepts in this book are a quick dip of the toe. You will benefit greatly from exploring some of them deeper on your own, especially some of the family systems concepts like differentiation. When we teach these concepts to our church staff, differentiation is the one our students struggle with the most, yet is the key to many of these breakthroughs. I trust that after you put this book down, you will continue your learning journey.

For all of us, my prayer as I was writing this book was for deeper experiences of freedom and grace for my readers. This world needs all the healthy leaders it can get. Leadership can be a lonely endeavor that is exhilarating and exhausting at the same time. Christian leadership is ultimately about God and other people, so my prayer is that you would find benefit in these tools to widen your leadership scope and deepen your leadership capacity. That you could move from reactivity to proactivity and create healthy culture while experiencing health yourself. It is no small prayer and I would love to hear how you're doing on your journey.

Thank you for taking the time to navigate these tools, and in closing, I will leave you in the hands of the wonderful Benjamin Zander, conductor of the Boston Philharmonic Orchestra. Ben says, "You can't impose your will on people's hearts. You can impose it on their hands and feet, but you can't win their hearts with force . . . you can subject them to your will and get results. . . . but their eyes don't shine. . . . my power is enormous but it exists entirely in my ability to make other people powerful."[2]

May you go in the peace and power of God's Holy Spirit.

DISCUSSION QUESTIONS

1. Failing seven out of ten times in baseball can make you a fortune! How do you handle your failure ratio and how high do you reset your expectations as you try some of these tools?

2. Have you experienced any of the three stages of leadership development (thrust into leadership and ill-equipped, burned by the organization you love, constantly adjusting to organizational and cultural changes)? Is one of these stages particularly poignant for you, or are you in one now?

3. One way a leader grows is to lead something she knows nothing about. What might this look like for you?

4. Following Jesus is not as tangible as it was when the disciples were alive. How do you discern God's direction? What do you do when you are wrong?

5. Christian leaders lead *from* their gifts and *through* their platforms. They don't say, "Because I'm in charge, that's why," but rather they recognize the unique gifts God has given them to lead. Why do people follow you? What is it about you that people want to follow? How might you appropriately develop this?

6. How have personality profiles helped you in your leadership? How might they have hindered you?

7. How can your friends pray for you right now?

ACKNOWLEDGMENTS

I am the recipient of an abundance of grace that I cannot describe in words, but I can describe in names.

Thank you, Mum and Dad, for raising me with a sense of adventure and a strong sense of right and wrong. Thank you for being overtly proud of me.

Thank you, Toni, for first introducing me to a life in Jesus, for being a true companion through challenging teen years and being such a force of encouragement.

Thank you, Lisa, for building a marriage with me that is the most life-giving relationship I have ever experienced. Living with you is such a grand adventure.

Bryson, you bring a rare combination of quiet strength, wicked humor, and easygoing skill. I am so enjoying watching you navigate into adulthood.

Andrew, you are equal parts party and compassion. You have a hair trigger, always ready to drop everything to help someone in need or have a good time.

Kaylee, you are the most organized artist, or the most artistic planner I know, and your heart is huge.

Many of my friends have encouraged me to publish along the

way, but I am particularly grateful to Sherry and Geoff Surratt for nudging me to submit a proposal to Leadership Network.

Thanks to Greg Ligon and Joey Paul for giving me the opportunity to publish my thoughts with such respected organizations.

Thanks also to Matt Manning for reading an early draft so carefully and giving such insightful edit suggestions.

And finally, thanks to Jesus of Nazareth for a good news that is so much better than I thought and for continuing to show me greater depths of freedom.

FURTHER RESOURCES

This book is an overview of concepts that deserve more treatment than space allows. I took a page or even a paragraph for several concepts that could justify a book-length treatment or require considerable time to implement.

For those who wish to dive in deeper, or go through these materials in a group, I have provided additional resources at stevecusswords.com. You can find a set of videos that explain each key concept in more detail so you can watch the videos as a group, or individually, before you gather to discuss. Group facilitators will find a facilitator guide with some extra tips on guiding groups safely through what can be some vulnerable material. The website also has a downloadable verbatim template and a link to a genogram app for those wishing to try those tools.

I love hearing from you. You can find me in all the usual social places: Facebook, Twitter, and Instagram.

NOTES

Introduction
  1. James Thurber, "The Shore and the Sea" in *Further Fables for Our Time* (Mandarin Press, 1991).

Chapter 1: The Anxiety Gap
  1. The John Maxwell Company, "7 Factors That Influence Influence," *The John Maxwell Co.* (blog), July 8, 2013, http://www.johnmaxwell .com/blog/7-factors-that-influence-influence.
  2. Marcus Buckingham, *Primal Leadership: Learning to Lead with Emotional Intelligence* (Harvard Business Review Press, 2004), 63.
  3. RedCapeRevolution.com.

Chapter 2: Anxiety, Freedom, and How the Gospel Works
  1. Thomas Merton, *New Seeds of Contemplation*, 40th anniversary ed. (New York: New Directions, 1972), 34.
  2. James Finley (ed.), *Merton's Palace of Nowhere* (Ave Maria Press, 2018), 10.
  3. Eugene Peterson, *Eat This Book* (Eerdmans, 2006), 108.

Chapter 4: Idols, Vows, and the Stories We Tell Ourselves
  1. Jeanie Duck, *The Change Monster* (Three Rivers Press, 2001), 143.
  2. Tim Keller, "Preaching the Gospel," Reform and Resurge Conference, May 2006, Session 7.

3. Tim Keller, "Preaching the Gospel."

4. Jim Herrington, from handout given to me at a Faithwalking Retreat, 2014.

Chapter 6: Applying Family Systems to Leadership

1. Edwin Friedman, *A Failure of Nerve* (New York: Church Publishing, Inc., 2017), 14.

2. Friedman, *Failure of Nerve*, 14.

3. Roberta Gilbert, *The Cornerstone Concept: In Leadership, In Life* (Leading Systems Press, 2008).

4. Scott Wyman, https://scottwyman.com/Scott_Wyman /Differentiation.html.

Chapter 7: Tools That Diffuse Anxiety

1. "The Spiritual Side of Sleep," *Relevant Magazine*, https://relevant magazine.com/life/whole-life/features/2354-the-spiritual-side-of-sleep.

2. Colin Powell, *It Worked for Me: In Life and Leadership* (Harper Perennial, 2014).

3. Edwin Friedman, *Failure of Nerve*, 65.

4. Friedman, *Failure of Nerve*, 64.

Chapter 8: Genograms: What Has Been Handed Down

1. Seth Godin, "It's Not Your Fault," https://seths.blog/2015/11/its-not -your-fault/.

2. Murray Bowen, *Family Therapy in Clinical Practice* (J. Aronson, 1978), 383.

Chapter 10: A Wider Scope and a Deeper Capacity

1. Chris Seidman, *Jesus Creed* (blog), http://www.patheos.com /blogs/jesuscreed/2018/02/07/dark-chris-seidman/#SJ53R1Hkg VTGSC1Z.99.

2. Benjamin Zander and Rosamund Stone Zander, *The Art of Possibility* (London: Penguin, 2002).

BIBLIOGRAPHY

Here is a topical bibliography for further research.

FAMILY SYSTEMS THEORY

Friedman, Edwin. *A Failure of Nerve*. Seabury Books, 2007.

———. *Generation to Generation*. New York: Guilford Press, 1985.

———. *Friedman's Fables*. New York: Guilford Press, 1990.

Gilbert, Roberta. *The Eight Concepts of Bowen Theory*. Leading Systems Press, 2006.

———. *Extraordinary Leadership: Thinking Systems, Making a Difference*. Leading Systems Press, 2006.

McGoldrick, Monica, Randy Gerson, and Sueli Petry. *Genograms: Assessment and Intervention*. New York: W. W. Norton, 1999.

Napier, Augustus. *The Family Crucible*. New York: Harper Perennial, 1988.

BRIEF THERAPY, CYBERNETICS, AND CHANGE THEORY

Fisch, Richard, and Karin Schlanger. *Brief Therapy with Intimidating Cases*. San Francisco: Jossey-Bass, 1999.

Watzlawick, Paul, John Weakland, and Richard Fisch. *Change: Principles of Problem Formation and Problem Resolution*. New York: W. W. Norton, 1974.

NARCISSISM AND DIFFICULT PEOPLE

Cloud, Henry, and John Townsend. *Boundaries*. Grand Rapids, MI:
    Zondervan, 1999.
Meier, Paul, and Robert Wise. *Crazy Makers: Getting Along with the
    Difficult People in Your Life*. Nashville, TN: Thomas Nelson, 2003.

OTHER HELPFUL TOOLS TO
UNDERSTAND YOURSELF

Brown, Brené. *I Thought It Was Just Me*. Gotham, 2007.
Chestnut, Beatrice. *The Complete Enneagram: 27 Paths to Greater
    Knowledge*. Berkeley, CA: She Writes Press, 2013.
Cron, Ian M., and Suzanne Stabile. *The Road Back to You*. Downers Grove,
    IL: InterVarsity, 2016.

LEADERSHIP BOOKS WITH A SIMILAR
EMPHASIS ON SELF-AWARENESS

Clinton, J. Robert. *The Making of a Leader: Recognizing the Lessons and
    Stages of Leadership Development*. Colorado Springs, CO: NavPress,
    1988.
Herrington, Jim, Robert Creech, and Trisha Taylor. *The Leader's Journey:
    Accepting the Call to Personal and Congregational Transformation*.
    Wiley, 2003.
Scazzero, Peter. *The Emotionally Healthy Leader: How Transforming Your
    Inner Life Will Deeply Transform Your Church, Team, and the World*.
    Grand Rapids, MI: Zondervan, 2015.

ABOUT THE AUTHOR

S teve began his leadership journey at a ranch for teens who were struggling with life issues. After college, he served as a chaplain at a level-one trauma hospital, then a youth minister in rural Appalachia, and a community outreach pastor at a large church in Las Vegas.

By far his most challenging leadership assignment is his current one: lead pastor at a suburban church. Since 2005, Steve has served Discovery Christian Church in Broomfield, Colorado. Discovery is an innovative and entrepreneurial church that has grown from 150 to more than 1,000 in weekly attendance. The church intentionally welcomes spiritual seekers and skeptics and is passionate about partnerships that break the local and global poverty cycle.

Steve has sixteen hundred hours of supervised ministry in clinical pastoral education and he holds a master of divinity from Emmanuel Christian Seminary. His thesis focused on the Hebrew Scriptures' dignity laws in Leviticus and Exodus. Steve encourages churches to consider ways they can tithe their property for the chronic needs of their communities. He is currently leading Discovery Church in a bold initiative to give half their land away for the chronic needs of the city. He loves leaders and has a particular concern for church leaders and their ongoing health.

Steve was privileged to grow up in Perth, Western Australia, in an adventurous family of origin. After moving to the United States for theological study, Steve married Lisa and together they have two sons and a daughter. When Steve isn't working, you can find him laughing with his family, knee-deep in a trout stream, or trying a guitar he cannot afford at a local music store. You can follow Steve at stevecusswords.com.